C000008717

The author of this well-writ
and vulnerability to enco
raise adopted children. Sh
pens a heartfelt book that is much needed in the Christian
community today. The result? A captivating account that
magnifies God's grace and teaches all of us the necessity of
learning to trust the Lord again and again.

ROBERT A. PETERSON,
Professor of Systematic Theology,
Covenant Theological Seminary, St Louis, Missouri
and author of *Adopted by God: From Wayward Sinners to Cherished Children*

This is a compelling story, but it is so much more because
Twila skillfully tells it in the context of the Redemption Story.
She uses her story to show us Jesus, so the truths are transfer-
able to give us hope in our own situations and relationships.
This is storytelling at its finest.

SUSAN HUNT,
Pastor's wife, former Director of Women's Ministry for the PCA
and author of several books for women and children

I had the privilege of watching the story of Carl's homecoming
unfold several years ago while we were part of Twila & Jeff's
church family. We had adopted an infant and already felt
a passion for orphan-care, so to watch that fire ignite in
their hearts, and not for a baby, but for an older child from
a country notorious for its difficult adoption process, was
awesome and moving to us. Not only that, but Twila and Jeff
are two of the most authentic Christ-followers I've known,
loving and serving their community with humility and
honesty. Twila's storytelling and insight into the older child
adoption journey is going to be an invaluable gift to many,
not only because of the uniqueness of their family and story,
but because of the knowledge and application of scripture
she brings to her writing. Her book won't just tell her own
story but will come alongside of others in their own stories,

helping them to ask good & necessary questions and to seek God every step of the way. I'm grateful for her courage to adopt and equally grateful for her courage to write about it.

CHRISTA WELLS,
Singer/Songwriter, Raleigh, North Carolina
www.christawellsmusic.com

"WOW", I just finished reading *Whispers of Hope* and I am sitting here filled with hope and encouragement. It was like sitting with a friend who shared her story with humility, transparency and realistic truth. I could relate with her on so many levels. This book comes alongside the reader to encourage perseverance, and to dig deep into God's word as the true source of strength, wisdom, perseverance and HOPE! I highly recommend this to everyone.

EILEEN MESTAS
www.morethanicanhandle.com
Forgotten No More Orphan Ministry
Mustard Seed Faith Ministry

Here is a first-hand account of an adoption by a family within our congregation. What you'll read is an honest, engaging and spiritually enriching story: not only is this book insightful, it reads like an adventure novel! I was personally encouraged and challenged throughout the process as the Miles Family pursued and adopted Carl. For all who seek insight into the journey of adoption, I strongly and enthusiastically recommend this book. Come be refreshed by its spiritual wisdom and genuine transparency! You'll be glad you did.

SCOTT COOK,
Pastor, Christ Our Hope Presbyterian Church,
Wake Forest, North Carolina

Twila Miles

WHISPERS

Finding Perspective
Post Adoption

OF

HOPE

CHRISTIAN
FOCUS

Unless otherwise stated, Scripture quotations taken from the *Holy Bible, New International Version*. Copyright © 1973, 1978, 1984 by International Bible Society. Used by permission of Hodder & Stoughton Publishers, a member of the Hodder Headline Group. All rights reserved. "NIV" is a registered trademark of International Bible Society. UK trademark number 1448790A

Scripture quotations marked (ESV) are taken from the *Holy Bible, English Standard Version*, copyright © 2001 by Crossway Bibles, a division of Good News Publishers. Used by permission. All rights reserved.

Copyright © Twila Miles 2015

paperback ISBN 978-1-78191-682-7
epub ISBN 978-1-78191-702-2
mobi ISBN 978-1-78191-703-9

Published in 2015
by
Christian Focus Publications Ltd,
Geanies House, Fearn, Ross-shire,
IV20 1TW, Great Britain.

www.christianfocus.com

Cover design by Moose77.com
Printed by Bell and Bain, Glasgow

MIX
Paper from
responsible sources
FSC® C007785

All rights reserved. No part of this publication may be reproduced, stored in a retrieval system, or transmitted, in any form, by any means, electronic, mechanical, photocopying, recording or otherwise without the prior permission of the publisher or a licence permitting restricted copying. In the U.K. such licences are issued by the Copyright Licensing Agency, Saffron House, 6-10 Kirby Street, London, EC1 8TS www.cla.co.uk

Contents

Dedication

This book is dedicated to my son, Carl.

Every time I look at you, I find myself filled with awe that God would bless us so richly by bringing you into our family. You add so much joy and meaning to the Miles household! Thank you for sharing your life with us.

All my love, Mom.

Acknowledgements

I am utterly amazed by the love and compassion our Lord Jesus Christ has for His people. It is no wonder that He planted the idea for this book in my heart shortly after we adopted. He knew that adoption is often challenging, and He wanted to give hope and encouragement to struggling parents. I don't know why He chose me to be the one to put these words of hope down on paper, for I am not a perfect mother; but I do love Jesus, and I give Him all the credit for any good that may come from this book.

I would be remiss if I did not give credit and appreciation to Carl, the son God brought into our family through adoption. Right from the start, Carl understood the importance of the message in this book, and he willingly allowed me to document many of the challenges he experienced in order to help other adoptive families thrive. He is such a compassionate and brave young man, and I deeply love and appreciate him.

Then there is Jeff, the man I have been madly in love with since we were teens. Not only has God allowed us to share our lives together as husband and wife, but He has also brought us closer into relationship with Him as He walked with us through both the dark and sunny days. I love you,

Jeff, and am thankful for the many times you took care of the children so I could go off by myself to write. Then, as I completed each chapter, you took the time to read through every page, offering your thoughts, advice, and corrections. This story is not mine alone, but one that we share.

Of course, I must also give thanks to the rest of our children, Abigail, Jeffery, Felicia, and Madison. All of you prayed for Carl before he entered our family, and then you openly accepted him as your true brother once he came into our home. Thank you for allowing me to record some of your stories in this book as well, for you, too, play important roles in this adoption journey.

Then, to my parents, Carl and Eugenia Welch, and my sister, Gena, I extend my love and gratitude. All of you have given your lives to the Lord Jesus Christ and openly share Him with people around you. You are such strong examples of what it means to be lights in this dark and hurting world. I hope you know how much your love and encouragement have meant to me as I endeavored to write my first book.

To my dear Book Chicks, you are so much more than a book club to me. You are my closest friends, and a constant source of laughter, strength, and encouragement. You were some of the first people to find out our plans of adoption. From the very beginning, you surrounded my family with the love and support we needed. Thank you. I love you girls more than I can express.

Christ Our Hope Presbyterian Church, our family has been incredibly blessed by you. Your prayers and support for me as I wrote this book were such beautiful gifts that I treasured. Not only that, but as I found myself needing a quiet place to study and write, you provided for me a desk with a view, as well as a library full of theological books in which I immersed myself for hours on end. But more than anything, I am thankful that when we brought Carl into this part of the world, you opened your arms and readily accepted him as part of our church family.

Dr Robert Peterson, not only did I sit under your tutelage at Covenant Theological Seminary, but I also had the great privilege of having you as my writing mentor. I remember how nervous I was to have you read one of the chapters in this book, because you had the reputation of being completely honest with writers, and I was not sure how you would respond to my work. I must say that your encouragement, prayer, and help in seeking a publisher were a humbling experience for me. I never expected so much from you, but am eternally grateful for all you have done to help make this book a reality.

Willie MacKenzie, you exemplify how a Christian publisher ought to live and work in the literary world. Every email I received from you, even before taking on this project, was helpful and kind. Christ was reflected through you in every exchange we had. You demonstrated great patience as I sent question after question, and always treated me as a sister-in-Christ rather than simply a project. I prayed for months that God would link me up with just the right publisher for this book, and I am thankful that He worked out all the details so that you and the other folks at Christian Focus Publishing would be the people I would be blessed enough to work with.

And last, but not least, I would like to say thank you to Rebecca Rine, my editor. You, too, were lifted up to God in prayer months before you were ever assigned to this book. I asked God to provide just the right editor who would help make God's messages in this book shine. You proved to offer even more than I had hoped for. It is obvious that your own walk with the Lord affects how you view all of life. You are gentle and kind in personality, as well as gifted and wise with the use of words. I am thrilled that you have played a part in shaping the final outcome of this book.

Preface

WE have a son, Carl, who was adopted five years ago at the tender age of twelve. He faces deep internal battles almost daily from the abuses he endured during his orphan years. These sufferings have taught him to cling tightly to his survival instincts, and to build strong walls around himself in an effort to prevent further hurt from entering his life. Even though he has a kind heart, his insecurities swirl in his head, causing him, on occasion, to unintentionally leave a wake of heartache behind him, pushing away many of those who love him and want to help.

When he initially entered our home, we had hoped and expected that he would find refuge, love, and peace in the midst of his new family. Years later, however, wars continue to battle within him, stealing away the peace and security we long for him to experience. Beneath his tough exterior lies a heart that wants to fit in, but keeps questioning everything foundational to his life. He wonders if he is truly loved, or is that just something we tell him? He questions whether or not he belongs here, because life is not easy for him. And he seems to be expecting a day when we will disown him as a son. The pain returns with each cutting word he throws our way.

Carl was abandoned by his first set of parents, so perhaps it is not surprising that he experiences no security with his second set. As insecurities such as these arise, Carl often responds by pushing all of us away, especially me, his mother. When his defenses go up, he tells me how much he does not like me, and that he wishes I had never come into his life. Logically, I know fear and anguish are consuming him, and I want to help him; but, emotionally, the continual darts being thrown my way pull me to my own place of pain and heartache. During these intense moments, I find that Carl is not the only one needing help to continue on; I, too, need an extra measure of strength and support.

For years, I devoured book after book, seeking the help and personal encouragement I yearned for. What I found, though, was a host of wonderful books geared toward helping the adopted *children* of this world, but none that spoke directly to the struggles adoptive *parents* often go through when trying to reach a broken child. From that platform, God began to compel me to write this book in order to fill that void. Unlike most adoption books, *Whispers of Hope* is unique in that it does not explain how to adopt a child, nor does it provide a comprehensive method for rearing an adopted child. Instead, this book offers something desperately needed in the adoption community: *Hope for adoptive parents who are struggling more than they ever thought possible.* Not knowing how to help a traumatized child learn to trust, love, and connect in a family unit can lead to discouragement and even despair for the entire family. *Whispers of Hope* was written to give encouragement, new perspective, and hope through Jesus Christ to the adoptive parents who feel like they are drowning in this endeavor, needing a life-line. This book urges parents to seek the Lord in the midst of their struggles, for He loves to rescue, restore, and redeem broken lives. Christ is the One who is able to pull anyone out of the mire of discouragement and despair, giving vision and hope for a stronger future.

My prayer for you is that God will speak to you in new and refreshing ways as you go through the pages of this book. Not every circumstance described here will match yours. But I hope that the stories and meditations in these chapters will shed light on your own situation despite the differences. One simple way you will see this is that I use the male voice and pronouns when referring to adopted children throughout this book. I did this simply because it made the book flow smoother, and because our adopted child is a boy. If you adopted a girl, however, I urge you to input the female voice when reading. And if there are other scenes that are different but parallel, use your imagination to extend the thoughts in this book into your own life and calling as an adoptive parent.

Also, on a closing note, please know that this book was written with Carl's blessing. We have had many conversations together, talking about our continued trials as well as the various experiences that ended up being included in this book. Carl is very courageous in allowing many of his own personal struggles to be put into print for the world to see. When I asked him why he was okay with my doing that, he simply said that he hopes our experiences will somehow be used to help other families grow closer as they work through their own challenges. I couldn't agree more.

Interview with Carl

AS I was in the process of writing this book, I asked people whom I love and trust to read it and to give me honest feedback. As that happened, I found that one particular question kept coming up in people's minds: 'What about Carl? Does he know that you have included some of his struggles in this book for everyone to see? *Is he okay with that?*'

In hearing that question repeatedly come up, I thought it may set people at ease if they got to know Carl a little bit before diving into the book. So, here is a conversation I recorded one evening between the two of us, shortly before he turned seventeen. Not only has he given me permission to publish the personal accounts in this book, but his tender heart genuinely hopes that the words given will, in some way, help other families thrive. I can't begin to express how thankful I am to Carl for his selflessness in this.

What happened in your life to cause you to become an orphan?

I can't really answer that question because one day I just woke up, and I was in an orphanage. And then I just moved on with it. As I go, I start remembering how I got there. I was taken away by cops because my parents were drinkers and did drugs, and my dad started doing those things, and that's when the cops took me, and then I just started moving around, orphanage to orphanage. Yeah, that's how I left.

Do you remember how old you were when you were placed in an orphanage?

Probably like six.

You have been in three orphanages throughout the course of your life. Do you remember back when you were in that first orphanage? When you were little, real little, did you ever think you would return to your first family?

No.

Did you think that you would be adopted by another family?

No.

Even when you were really young, you didn't?

No.

Really? Why not?

I didn't know God at that time. The only time I really knew I might be adopted was when Marina (a missionary who visited the orphanage often) came for the first time to the orphanage I was in, and that is how it all started.

So, what does knowing God and thinking you'd be adopted have to do with each other?

I don't know. I just started believing in Him and praying. Then, I had a lot of letters coming in from families, with the possibility of getting adopted, and I would hope for that.

So you prayed to get adopted?

Yeah.

Do you remember when friends of ours hand-delivered you the letter from us, telling you that we were going to adopt you?

Yes, it was when they came to adopt their own children. They had some things to do, and then they said, 'We have something for you.' And I got excited. I thought it was a present or something. After we got done with our fun thing, then they gave me the letter, and I read it. I cried. They happened to video-tape it, and that was pretty awkward.

Do you remember what you thought or felt when you read it?

I was just happy. I was like, okay.

Was it ever a scary thought, to be adopted?

Yeah, people started telling me that if I get adopted, I should run away, because they will, like, cut me up eventually, and sell my organs for money and stuff.

Were you ever concerned about going to another country?

No.

That didn't bother you?

No.

You are a brave soul. Aside from people telling you that we would cut you up and stuff, did you have any other fears?

No.

You didn't have any siblings before you came here, right? None that you know of, at least.

No.

Was it initially easy for you to feel like you fit in to your new family?

Yeah. I wasn't afraid or anything. I was actually excited.

We were excited for you to join the family, too. It wasn't always easy, though. Do you remember that you and I had lots of arguments that first year you were here? We didn't fight very much the first few months, but after about four months, it became a daily thing for us. Do you remember that?

Yeah.

Why do you think we argued like that?

Because I always argued with people back in the orphanage because that was just the way it was. Either somebody does something, or starts an argument. I had been there so long, that I got used to it, and I guess it just transferred.

It wasn't just your fault that we fought like we did. It was just as much my fault. We both had a lot of learning and growing to do. Did you ever think that your daddy or I would hurt you?

No.

Now, if you fast-forward to today, we still aren't perfect, right? No two people are. But how would you describe our relationship now?

Better than it was. We are closer. I used to not want to hang out with you, but now it's okay.

Okay, we are going to kind of jump back and forth from life here, and life there. We all have struggles and challenges in our lives, right? If you think back to the years before you were adopted, what is something you remember that was really good?

Marina (the missionary) was the best part.

She was pretty special to you, huh?

Yeah.

What was one of the hardest parts about being in an orphanage?

Everything! It's like, you have to look out for yourself all the time.

Why?

I mean, there were some nice people who would share with you, but some people would fight you for something that they don't have, but you do, and they just take it away easily. It's like surviving. Or, like, there is a drug addict who would walk around, then do some stupid thing and chase this orphan and try to kill him. It's pretty dangerous. It's like surviving.

The second day we met you in the orphanage, you told us there were three things that every orphan wanted.

I don't remember that.

You said every orphan wants food to eat, not to be hurt anymore, and to have a family. What do you think about that now?

Yeah, I would still say the same.

I thought that was pretty wise. Did you ever wonder if we would be able to love you as much as we love the other children? Was that ever a concern?

Sometimes, no. Sometimes, yeah. Actually, I think all orphans feel like they won't be loved as much.

As you know, you are a big part of this book, right?

Yes.

And you know that I have included in the book many of the hard things you have lived through, right?

Yeah.

I have included some of your own struggles, and some of mine. Are you okay with that?

Yeah.

Why are you okay with that? There are some pretty personal stories in there, you know.

Because people are going to read it, and they will need to know how to deal with their own, similar problems. I hope it helps families become stronger.

Me, too. Thank you, Carl, for being so courageous and honest in allowing me to share a part of your life with others. By doing this, I believe that you are, indeed, making a difference in this world.

1

Hopeful Beginnings

Following the Path of Adoption

AT times, memories surprise me like unexpected waves.

I'm sitting here on the back porch, watching my children and their friends play in the yard. My eyes land on Carl, and I am, again, consumed with awe and amazement that this child, from another country, is now living in our home, is an integral part of the family, is now our son. I have told so many people over the years that Carl was unexpected, unplanned—that we thought four children were all we would have, and that God surprised us with another. That was a lie, though. Not an intentional lie, but still an untruth in one sense.

Earlier today, when I first came out to the porch and was enjoying the soft breeze on my face, God whispered into my ear, 'Don't you remember? I have been preparing you for adoption for years.' 'What? I'm sorry, God, I'm not sure if I heard you right. What are you talking about?'

Immediately, as if an old projector had been turned on, I began to remember long-lost snippets of my life. Bits of conversations. Feelings. Thoughts.

The first one that came to mind occurred on a winter evening about four years ago. The kids were starting to get ready for bed when we looked outside and noticed it was snowing. 'Put your boots and coats on, kids. Let's go out and enjoy the snow!' It was coming down pretty hard, and since the temperatures had been below freezing for days, it quickly began to accumulate. I recall being mesmerized as I looked up to the street light so I could see how much snow was falling. The wind and flakes swirled around me, giving the evening a magical feel, like I was being swept up into the life of the snow. I looked over at Abigail, who was right beside me, with her tongue out, joyfully catching snowflakes. Felicia and Madison were twirling, with their heads back, getting caught up in their dizzy joy. And Jeffery had grabbed the little round plastic sled, excitedly journeying up and down the hill across the street from our house. Laughter from all pealed through the air, and I simply stood there, taking it all in. Some moments you just don't want to end.

A couple of our neighbors came out to play as well, and we ended up asking them to spend the night. The entire next day was spent joyfully playing in the winter wonderland, and when evening came, we did not want our friends to go home, so we asked if they could spend a second night with us. That's when it happened. That's when I remember God speaking to my heart. 'Twila,' He said, 'one day you will have this many kids in your home.' 'Yes, Lord, I can see myself having more children. I could do this. I would love for you to fill my home with more little feet, laughter, family.'

Then, as soon as that memory became crystal clear, God cut that tape and began a new film of a very different part of my life. I then found myself in the memory of one of the last conversations I had with Aunt Debby, my mother's little sister, shortly before she died of cancer. We were in the sunroom at Mom and Dad's beach house. Mom was on the bigger couch, and Debby and I were beside each other on the love seat. Our conversation was sweet, but bold and honest. Debby knew at that point that she did not have much time left to live, so we talked about heaven. She said she was not afraid to die because she knew she would be with the Lord, but she was sad to think about leaving her family, knowing how much they would grieve. She talked about her children, who were grown, and we prayed together for them, for their futures, and for the strength of their faith to continually increase throughout their lives. After saying 'amen,' she turned to me with that kind, gentle face, and asked me about my children. I caught her up on what was going on in their lives; then she, point blank, said, 'Twila, I bet you will adopt one day. I could see you doing that.' Rather than denying that possibility, I agreed with her that that just might happen sometime.

'Yes, Lord, I see that You planted many tiny seeds of adoption into my heart long before they came to fruition. You knew all along that our family was not yet complete. So, even though it seemed like the idea of adoption came up out of the blue, it didn't really, did it? Carl was planned long ago, even "before the foundations of the earth" (Eph. 1:4).'

On Sunday, February 28, 2010, we were visiting a friend, talking about our children, and catching up on our lives, when she asked me if I knew anything about summer hosting programs. She said that she had heard of a local group that was going to bring over orphans from Ukraine so the children could have the experience of spending three weeks with families here in the US. I was not familiar with the program, nor was I very interested in learning about it. I did not want to be rude to my friend, however, so I patiently listened to her as she excitedly shared what she knew. As this conversation came to a close, she offered to send me the link to the hosting group. I promised I would look at it, not because I was considering hosting, or adopting, but simply because I knew it would make my friend happy.

The next day, upon receiving the link, I almost deleted the email. Thankfully, though, I didn't. I decided I would be a good friend, and at least look at what it had to say. I opened up the site, clicked on the 'view orphans' link, and, immediately, our lives changed.

It's hard to put into words what happened at that moment, except to say that God opened my eyes to the fact that one of those children was supposed to join our family. Now, orphans have always tugged at my heart strings, but *nothing* like this had ever happened before. I remember crying … crying for those children, ages eight to sixteen, who were stuck in orphanages, without parents; crying for the hope that we were supposed to offer a home to at least one of them; and crying that the good Lord was nudging us—*us*—to have a part in doing this good and worthwhile thing called adoption.

I got up from the computer, went to talk to my husband, Jeff, and asked if he would ever consider adopting an older child from Ukraine. Amazingly, he said, 'Maybe!' That almost blew me over, because every other time in the past I had asked anything about adoption, he had said, equally quickly, 'No.' But 'maybe' was a word full of hope. He encouraged me to keep researching as much as I could about these children, and get back to him on what I found. So that is exactly what I did.

The next day, I had a wealth of information on the plight of Ukrainian orphans, so I shared what I was learning with Jeff. I had found all sorts of sad statistics, such as 'without intervention, upon leaving the orphanage [at age sixteen], 60 per cent of girls will end up in prostitution, 70 per cent of boys will be on the streets or in jail, and 15 per cent will commit suicide within the first two years on their own' (http://www.newhorizonsforchildren.org/). We talked about what it must be like to grow up without parents to love and guide you through life, and how the older children are typically passed over in lieu of the available babies. After we talked, I was ready to begin the adoption process, but Jeff simply asked me to keep researching and to continue informing him about everything I found out regarding orphans in Ukraine.

I was thrilled that Jeff was still interested in learning more about these children, but I wasn't so certain that he was drawn to adopt one into our family. So, I had to look him straight in the eyes and say, 'Please be completely honest with me on this. If you are wanting me to continue to dig deeper into this idea of adoption just because you think it will make me happy, I need you to tell me to stop. You see, it's important for me to know what you think about our adopting. If it truly is something you would like to pursue, then, great, we'll keep going. If you are going along with this just to appease me, however, then we need to stop. If we choose to do this, then it will have to be something that we decide to do together, for it is going to permanently change our family.' Amazingly, without hesitation, he said that given all that he knows now about these children, he cannot *not* adopt. If he turned his back on what God was calling us to do, then he knew we would regret it for the rest of our lives. So, the green light was on!

From that day of beginnings, we set our eyes on the horizon and sprinted toward the goal of bringing home our orphaned child. We did not meander slowly down this path, for God impressed on our hearts to **move**! God works uniquely in each family, but in ours He instructed us not to host a child, but to immediately begin preparing for adoption. We were not to look too closely at our finances to figure out how we would come up with the $30,000 to make the adoption happen. We were not to look to the future to figure out how we would put five kids through college, or how we would pay for weddings, or how we would be able to save for our retirement. God knew that if we fixated on those things, they would completely paralyze us, and we would never adopt this child. So, God said to move quickly, to run, to fix our eyes upon Him and His plan for this child, and to trust that He would show us how to go down this path.

Adopt: 'To take and rear (the child of other parents) as one's own child' (http://dictionary.reference.com/browse/adopt).

Adoption is not just about plucking someone out of a hopeless situation and rescuing him. It's about giving your very life to another. If you adopt, it will be one of the most selfless acts you have ever done. It will also be one of the hardest, yet one of the most worthwhile things you will ever experience. On the very first day that we met our adoption facilitator face-to-face, he looked us in the eyes and told us that even though we had four biological children, we were not to go into this thinking our adopted child would emotionally be just like our others. He informed us that the mere fact that the child we were adopting was an orphan meant that he had experienced significant trauma in his life. Chances are that he would bring fears and anxieties into our home, and we needed to start immediately equipping ourselves (through sources such as books, blogs, and talking to other adoptive parents) to understand where he was coming from, so we could begin to parent him in ways that he would need, in ways that would be effective and wise, yet in ways that would be humble and full of grace.

I hate to admit it, but in the past I would hear about orphans, feel sorry for them, then tune them out. I would simply keep living as if they weren't real, or as if it was up to someone else to do something about them. When God's timing was right for us to adopt, though, He grabbed hold of us and made it clear that we were to do something. No, we couldn't adopt all the orphans of the world, but we could make a significant difference in the life of one child. Not just any one child, but the one child whom He had chosen to be in our family.

That was the premise of our adoption. It wasn't based or begun on the foundation of what we had planned or envisioned for our family; it was begun by God Himself on the foundation of what He had planned for Carl (the boy we ended up adopting)—and for us. You see, all through the Bible, we are given stories about how God answers prayers. He is an intensely personal God and loves to make Himself known to His people. For years, in an orphanage in a tiny town in Ukraine, a little boy prayed to God, making his fears, requests, and desires known. As with all of us, he did not want to go through life unloved, ignored, forgotten. He didn't want to be invisible to the world. He wanted to be known, to be seen, to be loved unconditionally. He wanted to belong to a family, and God heard his cries, and delivered him.

Don't you love it when God gives you new perspective on something that you thought you already knew? As we prayerfully considered this directive of adoption in our lives, we initially focused in on James 1:27, which says,

> *Religion that is pure and undefiled before God, the Father, is this: to visit orphans and widows in their affliction, and to keep oneself unstained from the world* (ESV).

Early in this process, I knew that we were supposed to adopt, but that did not stop my fears from creeping in. I would vacillate between knowing for certain that this was what God desired for us to do and questioning whether or not we could do it. So God, in His eternal patience, began to teach us about His view of adoption so that we could better grasp the fact that He would faithfully lead us through the adoption process, as well as through the entire life of the child He had chosen for us.

This is how we know what love is: Jesus Christ laid down his life for us. And we ought to lay down our lives for our brothers. If anyone has material possessions and sees his brother in need but has no pity on him, how can the love of God be in him? Dear children, let us not love with words or tongue but with actions and in truth.

1 JOHN 3:16-18

In these verses, I clearly saw that Jesus laid down His life for us, and that we ought to do the same for other people, namely, we were to lay down our lives for this orphaned boy. We were to be willing to give up many of the material possessions we owned in order to afford to give this child a home. We were to show our love for Christ by being obedient to Him, and our love for this orphaned child, by our actions. We were, in essence, to be the hands and feet of Jesus to this young boy.

So, as we journeyed down the path of adoption, I kept envisioning myself as representing Jesus-in-the-flesh to this hurting, abandoned child. There was more for me to learn, though. On October 30, 2010, while in Ukraine, I wrote in my journal that Matthew 25:34-40 had taken on new significance for me. I'd like to share this Scripture with you, as well as my journal excerpt in response to it:

Then the King will say to those on his right, 'Come, you who are blessed by my Father, inherit the kingdom prepared for you from the foundation of the world. For I was hungry and you gave me food, I was thirsty and you gave me drink, I was a stranger and you welcomed me, I was naked and you clothed me, I was sick and you visited me, I was in prison and you came to me.' Then the righteous will answer him, saying, 'Lord, when did we see you hungry and feed you, or thirsty and give you drink? And when did we see you a stranger and welcome you, or naked and clothe you? And when did we see you sick or in prison and visit you?' And the King will answer them, 'Truly, I say to you, as you did it to one of the least of these my brothers, you did it to me.'

MATTHEW 25:34-40 (ESV)

In response to these verses, I wrote in my journal:

All this time I thought *we* were being the arms and feet of Jesus in going and loving these orphans. But as I read these verses today, I see the *orphans, too*, as representing Jesus. This tells me that Jesus permeates adoption. He is everywhere, present on both sides! How prideful was I to think that my part was the most important one. No, once again, God has reminded me that this is not about me at all; it's entirely about Jesus, for He is the one who not only loves the afflicted enough that He wakes us up to their plight so that we can help, but He also personally loves the orphans of this world. He doesn't just love them, He relates to them, He feels their pain of abandonment, He enters into their lives so much so that when we help them, we are in effect helping the very Son of God.

With that on my mind, adoption became very holy to me. I knew that God had fore-ordained this boy to join our family, and I wanted to honor God in how I (we) parented him. I was afraid of failure, but hopeful because I knew God, Himself, had called us to this task. No matter how weak or uncertain Jeff and I would be in helping this child, we knew that God would be our backbone, and that His plans would reign despite our fallenness.

When the day came to meet our son, Jeff and I were confident that we were exactly where God wanted us to be. I remember being in the director's office at the orphanage, waiting for Carl to step inside. I expected him to be timid and shy as he entered; but, instead, he burst into the room, with a huge smile pasted across his face, and with joy and expectation oozing from every movement. Immediately, his eyes found ours, and our hearts were connected for all time. He didn't know exactly what to do, so he went up to Jeff and extended his hand, which Jeff enthusiastically shook. Then he came to me, expecting to shake my hand, too, but I just *had* to hug him! He was a child of mine, and I wanted him to know how much he was loved from that first moment. I think I caught him off guard, though, for after the hug I noticed he was blushing. That made my heart melt even more.

Meeting Carl was sweet and wonderful. He was trusting, loving, and kind, and he stole our hearts from the very beginning. We spent a couple of weeks together, and bonded quickly. During this time, Jeff and I spent our evenings reflecting on, and marveling about, our experiences that each day offered. Not wanting to forget those memories, we were faithful to blog our journey on a daily basis (milesfamilyfun. blogspot.com). One night, as I was typing, I became overwhelmed with the reality of what was happening. We were not simply on vacation, making a new friend. We were in the midst of bringing into our home a child who we had only just met. But what an incredible child this was! Just that afternoon, for example, we had taken two large pizzas with us to the orphanage to share with Carl and his two best friends. We knew that pizza was something they rarely ate, so it would be a treat for them. What we didn't expect was the reaction of the other orphans as we arrived with the meal. In an instant, we were surrounded by a host of hungry children, begging to have a bite of the food we were holding. My heart ached for each of them. I remember looking over to Jeff, not knowing what to do. Carl, who had excitedly met us at the taxi when we first got there, took charge and beckoned us to follow him. He swiftly went into the room reserved for families and children getting to know each other during the adoption process. As soon as we entered, our translator gently closed the door, with a sea of hopeful faces remaining behind it.

Carl and his two friends immediately sat down at the table, and Carl offered up a prayer of thanksgiving. We lifted up the pizza box lid, and the boys quickly devoured the entire thing in record time. As they were finishing up their last few bites, I started to open the second pizza for them, but Carl shook his head, 'no.' With a gentle smile, he picked up the box, opened the door, and handed it to the other children, who were still waiting behind it.

As I finished blogging about that experience, I was touched with how tender-hearted this child was, how precious a gift he was to his friends in the orphanage, and how blessed we were to have him join our family. My emotions swelled, and I found myself pleading with God to be with Carl as he left his friends at the orphanage, and to help us as we brought him into our home. Over the course of the next couple of days, I wrote a poem, putting words to those thoughts and prayers.

FRAGILE

By: Twila Miles

Moving forward with God's purpose and plan,
To save a little boy in another land.
Counting the hours before we can give
A smile and a hug; a chance for him to live.

Finally we see him and his sweet, smiling face.
He is strong and courageous, yet fragile as lace.
Surrounded by friends he's full of joy and delight.
Games give us time to connect and grow tight.

Be with us, Lord, as he holds our weak hands.
To give him a foundation, not hopeless sand.
Well fed, cared for, in this temporary place,
But a real home he needs, filled with love and grace.

Timid and scared to leave this comfort zone,
But ready to change and move to a new home.
Restless, yet happy, each day closer to the new
Experience that shall carry him closer to You.

He now does what he can to remember his friends
Though some may come, too—some see this as the end.
This new life ahead is larger than imagined,
So now, more than ever, we need love and compassion.

Be with us, Lord, as he holds our weak hands.
To give him a foundation, not hopeless sand.
Well fed, cared for, in this temporary place,
But a real home he needs, filled with love and grace.

Two days before we went to court to make the adoption official, Carl shuffled over to his bedside table and pulled out a little bag, and gave it to us. This bag held absolutely everything that was important to him in life: letters people had written him since he had been an orphan, pictures, and a few items from our time together. Could you imagine packing up to move, and finding that all you have fits into a sandwich baggie? That night when we went home, I began to think about what he had given us: he had joyfully, expectantly, unreservedly given us his whole life, knowing that he was now a part of our family, and that we would take care of him, love him, guide him, and always be there for him. I started thinking, isn't that what God wants us to do to him? Doesn't He want us to completely, joyfully, expectantly, unreservedly give our lives to him? And here, all along I thought we were changing this little boy's life. Little did I realize just how much he would change ours.

That was the beautiful beginning of how our son, Carl, came to join our family. We were thrilled at the prospect of adding another child to our fold, and refused to believe that we would experience extreme challenges in raising him. We never voiced it out loud, but deep down we truly believed that enveloping Carl with a great magnitude of love would give him reason enough to trust and bond with us right off the bat. I assumed he would always be joyful and thankful to have been chosen to be in our family, that we would always be thankful for the gift that he was to us, and that within no time at all, we would be functioning as a strong unit.

Within a matter of months, however, our reality went from being rosy to dark, from being joyful to anxious, from being hopeful to despondent. Many nights I'd cry myself to sleep, seeing myself as a failure, uncertain how to parent Carl, and feeling completely alone in this task. I did not know of anyone else who had ever walked down the path of older-child adoption, so I didn't have anyone to glean wisdom and encouragement from. You see, our son had deeply engrained fears and ways of going through life that controlled his responses to situations. He began to do things like beating and bullying our other son, Jeffery, almost daily. And his lack of respect toward me sent him railing for hours on end when Jeff was at work. Many other things happened, too, which I will share with you throughout this book. My desire in doing so is not to put Carl down or to ridicule him, but to relate to many of you who are experiencing similar difficulties, and to share with you the hope we found in Christ every step of the way.

One day was especially challenging, and I began to wonder if we had completely taken away Carl's joy for life when we brought him to the U.S. He seemed to always be afraid, upset, or angry, so I couldn't help but question whether or not we had rescued him from one difficult life that he despised, only to place him in another. 'Lord, why is parenting Carl so hard? We love him so much, and want him to be happy in this family. Does he think we made a mistake by bringing him here, so far away from the only life and country he has ever known? Does he even want to be here? We need Your help, Lord. I don't know what type of help to ask for, though, but You know exactly what we need, don't You? Would You please give us some of that, whatever that may be?'

I thought for sure God's help would come in the form of changing Carl somehow. Maybe by taking away some of his fears, or by giving him a gentle spirit. God did not choose to change Carl at that moment in time, though; He chose to change *me* instead. He brought me out of the mire of self-pity, complaining, and fear, and set me on the foundation of God and His plan for Carl. He lifted my face toward Himself and gave me the gift of a new perspective. One full of renewed hope, grace and expectation. One that would allow me to keep heading forward despite the obstacles. One that would equip me to give glory to God for all the good that He *was* doing, and all that He *would* do in Carl's life.

After Carl had been in our home for about six months, there was one particular day when God blanketed me with peace and understanding. He endowed me with new vision—new perspective—as He brought two small, yet powerful, experiences into my life. The first one came about as I sat on the floor beside my bed, organizing a mountain of books that had accumulated over the previous few months. I like to group the books on my shelf topically, so I was taking the time to look at each one individually to ensure it went in its correct spot. I was about halfway through the pile when something caught my eye: a corner of a photograph that was peeking out of one of the books. I was curious what the picture was, so I pulled it out of the book and found myself staring into the eyes of a young Carl.

The photograph was one that the Ukrainian State Department of Adoption took when Carl initially entered the system, which meant he was a tender six years of age. He had rosy cheeks, big blue eyes, a cute little nose, and a timid smile revealing a mouth full of baby teeth. I stared at that picture for a long time, wondering things like, did he have anyone to rejoice with him when his first tooth fell out? What was he thinking and feeling when he was taken away from his parents? Did he expect to be adopted quickly?

As I continued to study his expression, it seemed to me that at that point in his life, Carl was sad, yet hopeful—perhaps relieved that someone helped him escape a traumatic past, and expectant that better days were ahead for him. Yes, Carl must have believed that one day another family would take him home and love him, and we ended up being the family that gave life to that dream. As the realization of that set in, I could feel God's grace cleanse and renew me. All of a sudden, I no longer saw the challenges we were having with Carl as bad things, but as indicators, reminders, of how much pain and abuse Carl had endured through the years. Yes, he wanted a family then, and he still wanted one now. We just had to be willing to be patient with him as he healed enough from his past so that he could trust us.

Then, later that afternoon, I had all five children packed in the back of our van as we headed to the store to buy a few things. I pulled into a parking space and was about to get out, when, from the back of the van, I heard Carl say, 'Wait, Mom. Remember when you and Dad first went to the orphanage, and I got to meet you? We were in the Director's office for a little bit, but then we went to that big room down the hall. Remember? For years, I had been dreaming of going in that room, getting to know my new mom and dad. It was wonderful. Then, the next day I thought you were coming back again at noon, just like you did on the first day. But you weren't there at 12:00, or 12:30, so I assumed you had changed your mind about me, and decided not to come back. I wish someone had told me that you would be coming at

2:00 that second day rather than noon, because that was the loneliest I have ever felt. I cried and cried, until I couldn't cry any more. Did you know that?'

No, I never knew that had happened, and my heart ached as I imagined him so sad. With tears in my eyes, I thanked him for sharing his experience with me. There had been so much turmoil in our relationship in the last few months, I had lost sight of the true issues at hand. I had been allowing my fears and emotions to rest on shaky ground based solely on the actions that I saw, but Carl's willingness to share with me, unprompted, a very personal, vulnerable part of his adoption experience helped me to see him more as the hopeful little boy I had viewed in the photograph earlier that day than the belligerent, out-of-control teenager that I often struggled with. Once again, I could sense God at work, helping me to understand Carl a bit better.

In just one day, God had brought me from being depressed and worried about the present difficulties that we were facing with Carl to being joyful and expectant about better days ahead. My own loving Father had refueled my drive to do whatever it would take to help Carl heal from his past, and grow into his future. That is just like God, though, isn't it? He is God of new life, resurrection, and hope. That is why I am writing this book. I'd like to offer renewed hope and encouragement to anyone who may be struggling with the harsh realities that often come with adoption. My prayer for you is that God will give you a new perspective on your child and the role you have been given as that child's parent. Most of all, however, I pray that God continually lifts your eyes to see His presence in your home. Your adopted child was brought there by the Lord for reasons you may not yet understand. Rejoice in being a part of His plans, and pray for patience, wisdom, and understanding as you travel down the path set before you. Know ahead of time that this road will be bumpy, but rough terrain does not mean we should travel down a different road. It just means that we will become stronger in the Lord as we lean into Him for guidance and support.

> *'For I know the plans I have for you,' declares the LORD,*
> *'plans to prosper you and not to harm you, plans to give*
> *you hope and a future.'*
> JEREMIAH 29:11

> *But may all who seek you rejoice and be glad in you;*
> *may those who long for your saving help always say,*
> *'The LORD is great!'*
> PSALM 70:4

Personal Reflections:

1. Read 1 John 3:16-18. Christ taught us how we ought to love others, with actions and in truth, by giving our lives to others, by serving. What specific ways are you being called by God to love and serve today?

2. Read Matthew 25:34-40. Do you see how Christ permeates adoption? He truly is active and present on both sides. Do you understand just how holy that makes adoption? If you are struggling greatly with your adopted child, and wondering how any of you will survive

this calling, prayerfully ask God to grip your heart with new perspective and renewed hope. Your outlook on life makes a world of difference.

3.   Read Psalm 70:4. Memorize this verse. On your most difficult days, ask God to bring these words to your heart and mind. Rejoice in the Lord, and praise Him for how He is using you in life. Be encouraged that He has not placed you on that road alone, but is right there with you at all times. Yes, He is great, and greatly to be praised.

4.   Read Jeremiah 29:11. Rest assured that God has not brought challenges into your home to hurt you or your child. Rather, He is in the process of working out something grand in both of your lives. I would like to encourage you to keep a journal or a blog so that you can record your life story, as well as the journey of your family as you go through the joys and trials of adoption. Years from now, as you look back, you will be able to see just how God worked all things out in marvelous and unexpected ways for your good, and for His glory.

2

God My Help

Seeing Christ More Clearly
through Difficulties

DECEMBER 19, 2010, was a day of great significance for our family, for that was the day when Carl first stepped foot on American soil, bearing a new name, taking on a new citizenship, and starting his new life as an integral part of our family. We were all giddy with excitement, and immediately wanted to share Carl with our world of friends and family. We whisked him away to Hickory, NC, to experience an overwhelming, high-energy Christmas with the grandparents, aunts, uncles, and cousins on both sides of the family. A week later, we took him to the tiny town of Mount Olive to watch a giant lit-up pickle drop to ring in the New Year. Then, without taking a breath, we drove ten hours down to Florida to celebrate the joys of a family reunion at Disney. Every adoption book I had read before bringing Carl into our home advised us to initially keep our newly adopted son sheltered, with very few stimuli, and even fewer visitors, until he was acclimatized to his new surroundings, in order to reduce his stress. Our family, however, has always been full of extended family, travel, and activity, so we chose to ignore the advice given to us. We were amazed at how happy Carl was, how much he thoroughly enjoyed each of the trips, and how well he was getting along with people who were introduced to him. So, after the Disney trip, upon returning home to Raleigh, we assumed that he would be able to handle meeting and playing with the neighborhood children as well.

Now, let me stop for a minute to give you a picture of our home. There is constant activity buzzing in our house, and a fairly constant stream of neighborhood kids who feel at home with us. We love children, and always dreamed of having a home where kids would know that our door was open to them at any time. Our house is unkempt and cluttered, giving evidence of the life that unfolds there. And, to us, it is cozy, full of music, crafts, board games, bikes, pets, and baked goods, all of which we love to share with the neighbors. Shortly after our trip to Disney, however, we began to realize how our lifestyle needed to be tempered a bit to give Carl a chance to relax and begin to learn how to build relationships, not only with us, but with surrounding friends.

Once the whirlwind of Christmas, New Year, and Disney passed, we settled back into our home and began to resume 'normal' life. It took me a couple of weeks to get Carl enrolled in school, so I used that time to get to know him better and to gauge how much education he had under his belt. I was aware that Carl had attended school in the orphanage and was happy to discover that not only did he have beautiful handwriting, but also that he was literate in the Russian language. At his then current age of twelve, however, the rest of his academic knowledge was equivalent to that of a second grader in America. He could add and subtract, and could multiply up to five, but he had never seen fractions, decimals, or any other math beyond the basics. Because of this, we knew he would have quite a bit of catching up to do in school. He also only knew about five words in English, so, as we progressed through each day, I pointed out various objects around us to begin to give him a usable vocabulary. I wanted learning to be fun for him, so I used methods I thought he might respond to, such as teaching him the words for colors using M&Ms and punch-bugs, and reading Dr Seuss books together to introduce him to the English alphabet.

After spending the majority of a week primarily with me, though, I began to think that Carl would enjoy getting to know some kids in the neighborhood. So, one afternoon, we invited over two girls who had been waiting anxiously to meet him. Everyone went to the playroom to hang out, and I went to my bedroom down the hall to work on some things, completely oblivious to the fact that at this stage in his life, Carl needed constant adult supervision. He was so outgoing and personable that it didn't even occur to me that he would have challenges relating to others. I did not realize that his norm for playing with other children was not really playing at all; rather, it was a constant demonstration of trying to be the top dog. As I look back, I can now see that being the biggest, toughest guy on the block was imperative at his orphanage in order to survive. So, naturally, Carl would bring those tendencies into his new environment, not in the spirit of being mean for cruelty's sake, but simply in an effort to relate to those around him, and to establish with his new friends that he was not weak and needy.

As I was typing on my computer that evening, I heard our friends scream, and then a door slam. Abigail and Jeffery burst into my room to tell me that Carl had tried to force our giant beanbag chair on top of their friends, making them think that Carl wanted to hurt them. In response, the girls ran away from Carl, and locked themselves in the nearby bedroom. Carl did not seem to understand the fear reaction that had happened with the girls, so his feelings of inadequacy began to rise. Then, when I tried to explain to him that he needs to be gentle with people, and not do things that may hurt them, he immediately became consumed with fear, and began looking for a way out. I remember how he darted down the stairs and out the front door, like a quick, frightened rabbit. I ran after him, but when I got past the door, I looked around and only saw darkness. My heart rate picked up as I began to think that this little boy who had been with us for only a matter of weeks might be lost. What if, in his fear, he had run away from our home and just kept running? How would we ever find him again? I kept thinking, he doesn't know our address or phone number yet, and he doesn't know how to speak English to ask for help when he calms down and wants to return! On top of that, there was slushy snow on the ground, and he had run out barefoot and without a coat. Not knowing what to do, nor what direction to even begin searching, I called all the other children in the house around me. Together we offered up a quick, yet desperate plea to God, asking Him to protect Carl, and to help us to find him. Then I barked out orders to everyone.

'Felicia, call your daddy and tell him he needs to come home from work immediately.'

44

'Madison, once Felicia gets off the phone, I want you and her to stay here at the house in case Carl returns on his own.'

'The rest of you, divide up into groups of two and fan out in different directions to look for Carl, but don't go beyond the neighborhood without an adult.'

So, within about a minute, we had covered the situation in prayer, and organized everyone into action. We knew that time was of the essence, so we headed out into the night, calling for Carl, keeping our eyes peeled for him, and continuing to pray for God's guidance. I remember thinking, 'Lord, You know exactly where our son is. Ease his troubled heart and bring him back to us, or open our eyes to see where he went. I know that once he calms down, he will realize just how cold and alone he is. Protect him from frostbite, please, Lord, especially on his feet, and bathe him in Your presence until he returns home. I need You, Lord.'

That day wasn't the only time I have felt anxiety and fear well up inside of me when trying to help my children. Feelings of inadequacy rise within me at times when I least expect them, unbidden and unwelcomed. God has allowed me to struggle many, many times in life, though, as He has grown and matured me. Sometimes when I get all tangled up in these challenges, I find myself trying to fix everything around me in my own power. I mess up horribly, and am reminded of how fallen I am. This brings me to the place where I, once again, realize how very much I need God's rule, guidance, and help in my life. I especially need Him to teach me His ways as I parent the children He has entrusted to me.

Come and see what God has done:
he is awesome in his deeds toward the children
of man.
Bless our God, O peoples; let the sound of his
praise be heard ...
For you, O God, have tested us;
you have tried us as silver is tried.
You brought us into the net;
you laid a crushing burden on our backs;
you let men ride over our heads;
we went through fire and through water;
yet you have brought us out to a place of
abundance ...
PSALM 66:5, 8, 10-12 (ESV)

These verses are comforting to me. In them we can see that God actively loves the children He has given us by the fact that He works in wonderful, personal ways in their lives. *'Come and see what God has done: He is awesome in his deeds toward the children of man.'* In fact, God loves these children so much that He is willing to place pressure on us *parents* in just the right ways to discipline us, to teach us, and to help us become the people we were intended to be, living out our calling of parenthood.

'Bless our God ... for you ... have':

* *'tested us.'* In doing so, God teaches us the value of knowing Scripture and trusting Him in order to pass these tests.

* *'tried us as silver.'* He knows that refinement cannot be done in the easy moments of life, but requires intense heat, pressure, and time. Through it all, the impurities of our

lives are filtered out so that we can better reflect His glory.

- *'brought us into the net.'* At times, He allows our lives to become entangled in sin and difficult situations so that we will see our great need for His help and deliverance.

- *'laid a crushing burden on our backs.'* He allows us to experience heavy burdens so that we can understand what it means when Christ tells us to cast our burdens on Him. In doing so, we are given the privilege of experiencing His sustaining power.

- *'let men ride over our heads.'* He even allows people to trample over us and to bring us low. That's okay, though, for as we cling tightly to Christ, we will find that He will one day bring us on high.

- *'we went through fire and through water.'* Both of these can be dangerous circumstances, which can seem impossible to escape from. But in Isaiah 43:1b-2, God assures us with these words: *'Fear not, for I have redeemed you; I have called you by name, you are mine. When you pass through the waters, I will be with you; and through the rivers, they shall not overwhelm you; when you walk through the fire you shall not be burned, and the flame shall not consume you'* (ESV).

Then my favorite verse, the one I cling to when I am in the midst of being tested, tried, entangled, burdened, overridden, and facing seemingly impossible situations: *'Yet you brought us out to a place of abundance.'* That's not to say that after we endure these hardships, God will fill up our bank accounts as a reward. No, what we gain is far greater than anything monetary. We gain a closer, more intimate relationship with our Lord and Savior, Jesus Christ. He moves from being an outward, impersonal example in our lives, to an inward, all-encompassing, deeply personal Redeemer. As this happens, our love for God grows, and we become malleable pieces of clay in His hands, which can be used for His exceedingly good purposes. In doing so, He helps us to fight the selfish tendencies that rage within us, and shows us the need to look up to Him with love and devotion, and then to look out to others with humility and grace. Willing servanthood flows from that frame of heart and mind, which is the essence of parenthood—giving yourself to another for their good and God's glory.

I know that the end of the day is a trying time for many children, including ours. Even so, I have always felt it is important to try to end each day on a note of love and assurance. I have to emphasize the word 'try,' however, because there are days when this just doesn't happen. Either I am too tired, or we are all too frustrated, and we end up going to bed with unresolved issues. On nights like that, I can't beat myself up, though, for we are not perfect, and, unfortunately, we can't expect every day to end as we would like.

Other times, however, I find that God gives me the strength and grace to enter into my children's rooms in order to connect with them. On days that have been especially difficult, I long to reduce their anxiety and to ease their pain. Carl is not the only one, though, who needs our extra care and attention from time to time. Our biological children, too, need space where they can voice their concerns and fears, for sometimes they feel like they are being pushed aside as we give the necessary time to help Carl grow and feel secure in the family. Because of that, I believe this one-on-one time is vital to their own growth, sense of security, and peace of mind. So, no matter which child I am tucking in at night, I do my best to give them my full attention, even if it is only for a few precious moments.

On nights when they seem open to talk, sometimes I begin our conversations by gently asking questions such as: 'Are you okay? Did you feel afraid earlier today? Alone? Unloved? Was there something you needed that I just didn't see or understand?' Sometimes questions like these are met with a terse statement of, 'I'm okay, Mom.' Other times we simply hug, understanding that the words are hard to find. And yet other times those questions launch us into wonderful, deep, searching conversations. I used to always push for these long, meaningful talks, but I have come to realize that *any* response is a gift, a link building our relationship.

When these deeper conversations do arise with Carl, he will often touch on various struggles from his past. I have begun to keep a journal with him, writing down experiences each day that he would like to hold onto, as well as recording joys and pains that he recalls about his life in Ukraine. I don't want him to completely shut out or lose those memories, for they comprised twelve years of his life. For many reasons, God allowed him to have those experiences as part of his life story. They have had a hand in shaping who he is today, and will somehow play a part in the future God has laid out for Carl tomorrow.

Some days when Carl is somber, he shares with me things that make my stomach turn, and my heart ache for him. Like many orphans, he experienced more pain and anguish in just a few short years than most of us will experience in a lifetime, and I can't help but ask God if all that pain was necessary. My motherly instinct kicks in, and I find myself wanting to shield Carl from his own past, to protect him from it, to take it away. Then that feeling of helplessness tries to work its way in again, and I begin to wrestle with an illogical notion that somehow I failed Carl in his past. I wasn't there to hold him, protect him, nurture him, and love him during those young, tender years. But, of course, I couldn't be there. 'You, Lord, though, never failed Carl, did You? As my mind tries to picture Carl in the dark places of his early life, I am thankful that You were there. The realization of that graciously eases my anxious heart, and fills it with Your peace. Somehow, Lord, You have assured me that during those years, You lavished Carl with Your very presence, continually filling his little heart with strength, and giving him the ability to hope for a better future. You were the ever-present father to my son during his orphaned years, protecting him, comforting him, and bringing him to where he is now. Psalm 10:14b and 17 says, '... *to you the helpless commits himself; you have been the helper of the fatherless ... O Lord, you heard the desire of Carl*' (ESV ADAPTED) [yes, I am personalizing this verse!]; '*you strengthened his heart.*' I need not worry about his past.'

'Actually, I have no reason to fret over his present or his future, either, for You are in those areas as well. No place, no fear, no experience will ever take You away from Carl.'

Who shall separate us from the love of Christ? Shall tribulation, or distress, or persecution, or famine, or nakedness, or danger, or sword? ... For I am sure that neither death nor life, nor angels nor rulers, nor things present nor things to come, nor powers, nor height nor

depth, nor anything else in all creation, will be able to separate us from the love of God in Christ Jesus our Lord.
ROMANS 8:35, 38-39 (ESV)

Some days I lose sight of God's working, mending, and molding Carl. And, quite honestly, sometimes I forget that it's not just Carl who needs God to work in his life, but that we all desperately, daily need His sustaining presence. Many days, God has to remind me that all of us who are His children are somewhere on the continuum of being refined, altered to the core, changed—of becoming people who reflect the goodness of Christ. At times, my mind wanders away from God, however, and when I start thinking I can figure everything out on my own, that is when I tend to get caught up in the day-to-day battles of life, and feel beaten down, tired, and useless to my family. Often, I don't know how to best settle disputes, discipline my children, or help them grow and mature in their relationships with God and with each other. On other days, the clouds part, and God's light shines so brightly on a situation that I am reminded that God is in control, working all things out to His will. Jeff and I are not parenting alone, but have our heavenly Father right in there with us, helping us. Why do we forget that at times?

For Carl's second Christmas with us, our family went to a Christmas tree farm to cut down a live tree. We had never done that before, so it seemed like a wonderful adventure to take! We loaded everyone up in the van and drove to the farm, with high expectations of coming home with the best, most beautiful tree we had ever had. We only had one rule about the choosing of the tree: everyone in the family had to agree upon it. I remember that as soon as we got to the farm, we excitedly started searching for our tree. Before long, Abigail and Carl fell in love with one tree, while Jeffery fell in love with a different tree. They were both wonderful trees, worthy of cutting down and joining our family. As our family tends to do, though, competition entered the scene, and Abigail and Carl stood by their tree, and Jeffery stood by his. No one was willing to bend to the other. So, we were at a stand-still. I could feel the tension rising, and I had visions of our ideal tree-finding day turning sour. As I thought through various ways to mediate this stand-off, I kept coming to not-so-happy conclusions. I suspected that if either one of those trees was chosen, then the other party would hold a grudge against the other, and the day would be a bust. And if I simply told them that they couldn't choose either of those trees, but needed to find another that they would agree on, then bitterness would enter the picture, and each side would blame the other for ruining their chances of bringing home the 'best' Christmas tree. So, what to do, what to do … .

I feel like that many days, not knowing what to do. I so want life to be happy that I find myself quickly getting down when the kids argue, or when I don't know how to parent in a certain situation. Jeff is a wise and gracious father to our children, but more often than not, the strongest conflicts occur right after school, before Jeff gets home. I have come to believe that Carl exerts an incredible amount of energy during the school day, trying to remain self-controlled and attentive. This task may seem simple to most children, but for Carl, it is daunting, because he feels stresses from every angle. He feels pressure to be 'normal' and to fit in, pressure to relate well with the other students and teachers, pressure to understand the English language, and pressure to remain in control of himself for hours on end. So, it is no wonder that when he comes home, he is often in an unstable frame of mind, primed to blow up at the smallest disagreement.

When Carl yells at me in response to something I have told him, and marches away from me with a fearful look in his eyes, I want to help him, but I don't know what to do. He has been with us for over two years now, and at times, when we are correcting him on some behavior, he still reverts to survival mode, quickly becoming emotionally unhinged. 'Lord, I don't know how to teach him to shake off these fears, and help him to see that he can trust us. When will he realize that we are never going to harm him? We won't lock him in a closet for days, or whip him with a rubber hose, or bash his head into a concrete wall … we just won't.' In many ways, Carl is moving forward, fitting in, doing well, making friends, and enjoying life. There is this underlying question, however, as to whether or not he will make it through the day without an episode. Now, I'm not saying that these episodes are bad, necessarily. I actually feel that they are essential for him to see that at some point he will need to face portions of his past, talk about them, and, ultimately put these experiences at the foot of the cross. Otherwise, they are just going to grow and eat him up. They will keep coming out as fear or anger, and they will continue to hurt his relationships in life. 'Please help him, Lord. Take away his fear, and help him to start seeing You as his source of strength and peace, because apart from

You, there is no peace, is there? Lead us, Lord, as we travel down these unstable paths, and give us Your wisdom on how we ought to best help our son.'

You know, I love it that God is a God of details, and that He cares deeply about every part of our lives. As we stood at an impasse at the Christmas tree farm, I prayed, and asked God to show us how to resolve the conflict over a tree. As soon as I said, 'amen,' God moved. He opened my eyes to the fact that Jeffery's tree had a red ribbon on it. What does that mean, I wondered? We quickly realized that a red ribbon meant that that tree had already been chosen by someone else. So, I told Carl and Abigail to go look at their tree to see if it, too, was taken. In a minute, they came running back, saying their tree, too, had a red ribbon. So, just like that, God dropped all those nasty possessive feelings, and we were back on track to find the perfect family tree. I was amazed at how quickly and beautifully God answered my prayer.

Then I heard Jeff yelling for us all to go to where he was, that he had discovered *the* tree. When we found him, he was standing at the base of a tall, deformed tree. At first glace, the kids weren't sure how to respond, for this wasn't what they had pictured. But then Jeff said this was a grown-up Charlie Brown Christmas tree, and it needed to be loved. If we didn't choose it, then no one would, and it would be left here all alone and sad. Immediately, everyone grew attached to the tree, and began to call it Chuck (short for Charlie Brown). Well, everyone except for Felicia, for she had chosen another tree. When she pointed out her tree to us, though, a bee flew out of it, and she decided she didn't like that tree after all! In fact, she decided to join in with everyone, and wanted Chuck to go home with us. Joy surged through me as I sat back and watched God work. 'Thank you, Lord.'

Now, as unexpected stresses come up, and I don't know which way to turn, I have a reminder that I can trust God completely to help me in life. Not only is He present, but He cares. What's more, He has all the answers, and His answers are vastly different from mine. If only I would always trust Him. 'Please, Lord, help me to trust You more. Hmmmm, isn't that the same prayer I pray for Carl, that he would trust us and You more, too? I guess we could all use some help in that area.'

It's rare for the storms of life to be expected. More often than not, they side-swipe us when our guards are down, and threaten to overtake us. To an older adopted child, such a storm may appear at a simple word of correction from a parent that he perceives as a threat, or from a sideways glance from a sibling that he interprets as hatred. Especially for a child who has experienced abuse or neglect, any number of things could trigger him to act as if his very life is in danger. To those of us who have never experienced such trauma, these responses may look odd, but to the child, extreme reactions are normal. In fact, in the past, they have always served to heighten his senses and even to help him escape or endure abuses.

Because these reactions have already been learned and cemented in his mind and body, we must be patient—very patient—with him as his eyes are slowly opened to the fact that his life is completely different now. He is no longer in danger, but in capable, loving hands. He no longer needs to survive on his own, but is in a supportive family environment designed to nurture him. He will never be abandoned again, but is rooted in his new home. These facts—and all of their implications—will not penetrate his heart, mind, and actions overnight. It will take time, maybe even years, before his reactions are changed to reflect the truths of his new reality.

On that day, when evening had come, he said to them, 'Let us go across to the other side.' And leaving the crowd, they took him with them in the boat, just as he was. And other boats were with him. And a great windstorm arose, and the waves were breaking into the boat, so that the boat was already filling. But he was in the stern, asleep on the cushion. And they woke him and said to him, 'Teacher, do you not care that we are perishing?' And he awoke and rebuked the wind and said to the sea, 'Peace! Be still!' And the wind ceased, and there was a great calm. He said to them, 'Why are you so afraid? Have you still no faith?' And they were filled with great fear and said to one another, 'Who then is this, that even the wind and the sea obey him?'

MARK 4:35-41 (ESV)

In this story, Jesus directed His disciples to go in a boat with Him to the other side of the lake, a distance of some thirteen miles. It was no surprise to Jesus that a storm would suddenly appear and surround them out in the midst of the water. The great gales were not threatening to Him, though, so He found a comfortable, soft spot, and laid down to nap, for He had been teaching all day and was tired. His disciples, however, were gripped with fear when they saw the storm approach. These men had lived around and worked on boats for years, so they knew the destructive potential that a storm like this possessed. Intense fear surged through them as they imagined their own boat's demise. '*And a great windstorm arose, and the waves were breaking into the boat, so that the boat was already filling.*'

In repeatedly studying this account of the storm that swirled around Jesus and His disciples, I have become convinced that valuable lessons were embedded in Jesus' response to the dire situation. Jesus had an amazing love for people, and consistently demonstrated how much He cared for them in the way He responded to their needs. I see this story as a tangible gift from which parents can learn when helping our children grow through intense, threatening moments of crisis.

Lesson #1: You, the parent, need to be the more mature person, the one with self-control, the one who does not respond in harsh ways to your child's intense actions when insults are thrown your way. Jeff and I know this, but often fail at it. We have to constantly remind ourselves that if we react to our child with anxiety and defensiveness, then that will only propel him into a greater state of fear and instability.

In a panic, the disciples ran to wake up Jesus, accusing Him of what they *assumed* to be true, '*And they woke him and said to him, "Teacher, do you not care that we are perishing?"*'

Had my children said that to me, I would have been tempted to retort, 'What do you mean I don't care about you? I am the one who feeds you, buys you clothes, and gives you a roof over your head. Of course I care about you! How dare you disrespect me like that!' Jesus, however, didn't say that.

In fact, He didn't say anything at all in response to the false accusations.

Carl, too, in moments of panic, has blurted out many things that he assumed were true, but were miles away from being correct.

'You are mean and don't care anything about me!'

'I don't need to listen to you. I am perfectly okay, and don't need to change anything in my life!'

'My first mother was nicer to me than you are!'

'I hate you, and wish I had never come here!'

'I hate this family. Life in the orphanage was so much better!'

Fear can bring out the worst in us. It sometimes causes us to say things we wouldn't normally say and do things we will later regret. Fear ignites the innermost parts of our brains that cling to survival and makes the rational areas of our minds incapable of responding until the perceived threat has passed.

Lesson #2: Jesus' personal preference was probably to continue resting, since He was tired. His desire to help, comfort, and teach His disciples, however, was greater than His wish to sleep, so He got up to address the issues at hand. Many times we, too, must make the conscious choice to get up and move toward our children to help them, rather than praying that their problems would just disappear on their own.

Jesus did not roll over and say, 'Can't you see how tired I am? Everything is fine. Just trust God. Now please go away and let Me sleep.' No, He got up and responded to the fears of His disciples with action and compassion. He knew, of course, what the source of their fears was (the storm), and He actively addressed that issue: '*And he awoke and rebuked the wind and said to the sea, "Peace! Be still!" And the wind ceased, and there was a great calm.'* This leads to our next lesson:

Lesson #3: Jesus' first action was not to rebuke the lack of self-control, fear, and panic of His disciples by yelling at them or correcting them. No, His initial action was to remove the point of stress, thereby easing their trepidations.

Of course, we are not God, so we are not able to do miracles like He did in calming the storm, but we *can* assess the situation at hand and make wise decisions that may help settle the fearful heart of our children. The actions we can take to do this are as numerous and varied as there are children in this world. For our family, though, they include actions such as:

- talking to our child calmly, being fully in control of the tone and volume that we use (this one is a must)

- sending friends home if the extra activity seems to be too much for our child

- distracting our child, leading him away from the point of stress and into different areas of interest

- removing him from the room to talk privately, reassuring him that everything will be okay, and that we are here for him.

Too often have I responded to Carl's fears and accusations with harsh words and swift discipline, only to serve to drive my son farther from me. In seeing this story of Jesus and His fearful disciples, though, the Holy Spirit has begun to teach me how to better reach my son, and how to ease his uncertainties. In the heat of an episode, I am to ignore the destructive words coming from him and not take them personally (this step is excessively difficult for me, though). I am to take a quiet moment to see what the situation *really* is about (What had made Carl afraid? What events led up to this panic? What was he fearful of?) and to do whatever I am capable of doing to diffuse the fire where it had ignited, rather than simply responding where I see flames.

This, of course, is not always simple, and his reactions do not always prove to have a straightforward explanation that I understand or see. Even so, taking a moment to let Carl know that we are there for him, that we are concerned for him, and that everything is going to be okay, can help divert the potential onslaught of an intense meltdown. My natural instinct is to either yell at him for treating others poorly, or send him to his room by himself to diffuse the anger and to get the stress away from me.

Christ, however, did not do either one of those things. Rather, He engaged in calming the disciples' fears, and kept them near to Him, allowing them to see and experience His love and security. Likewise, once we address what appears to be the trigger, the best thing we can do from that point is *not* to send our child away to his room for a time out, for that may reinforce deeply rooted feelings of abandonment. No, rather than send him away, how about trying to draw him near? Have him join you in whatever you are doing, or offer to go for a walk together. Look for ways in the middle of the trying times to build your relationship and to connect. It's not easy, but it is incredibly worthwhile.

The relationship, you see, is more important than the rules. Enjoy your child, and look for the good in him. It is there! Sometimes when you are weighed down by stress, all you can see is the negative. In fact, you may find yourself constantly focusing on things that he is doing wrong. Be careful not to do that. Change your view of him, and purposefully see and commend him for the positive.

Lesson #4: Not until after the storm had passed and everything was calm again did Jesus begin to teach His disciples valuable lessons. Trying to reason with them while the storm was still brewing, while they were still panicking, would have been a waste of time; for the ability to think rationally leaves us when we are in survival mode.

Once the situation had diffused and the waters were still, Jesus talked to His followers about their actions. '*He said to them, "Why are you so afraid? Have you still no faith?"*' I used to think these words were harsh and condemning, but now I see them as truthful words said with compassion and love. In other words, I can hear Jesus gracefully asking, 'Why are you scared? Do you not realize that God is in the boat with you? Have you forgotten what you have seen, experienced, and learned since we have been traveling together? Have you forgotten who I AM?'

I AM the Son of God.

I AM the One who has known you since before the beginning of time, and called you by name. I AM the One you felt compelled to follow.

I AM the Holy One who has all authority in heaven and on earth.

I AM the Good Shepherd who casts out evil.

I AM the Great Healer.

I AM the One who can forgive sins.

I AM the Great Physician who eats with sinners.

I AM the Lord of the sabbath.

I AM the One who loves to bring about restoration.

I AM the One who loves you in a deeply personal way.

And, I AM not only the One who creates the wind and the rain, but also the One who commands them to come forth or to cease.

So, again, I ask, why are you afraid? I am with you, watching over you, protecting you, leading you, guiding you, teaching you, and working all things out for your good and God's glory. Even if the boat had capsized, you still would have been in my care. Be calm. Be assured of *who I AM*, and know *who you are* because of the very fact that I am in your life.

You are my children whom I have chosen.

You are of great worth because you were created in the image of God.

You are men living out your God-given callings in life.

You are people who have seen miracles that I have done, attesting to who I am.

You are listeners who have heard the words of Truth that I have spoken.

You are not alone.

You are loved by me.

At this point in their lives, the disciples were still grappling with the reality of who Christ was. Even though they had spent time with Him and witnessed all that He had done up until that point, they still were maturing in their knowledge of the fact that Jesus was, indeed, God incarnate. '*Who then is he, that even wind and sea obey him?*' They were beginning to catch on, but the full realization of who Christ was, and who they were in Christ, had not yet sunk in. In many ways, they were infant believers whose eyes were slowly being opened to see and understand things that, on their own, they could never grasp.

As I read and reread this account of Jesus and His disciples, I am realizing many things. For one, when Carl is experiencing fearful, out-of-control times in his life, Christ is right there with him, even though Carl does not realize yet who is 'in his boat with him.' Likewise, when I start to feel stressed over how to help my son when he gets out of control, I can rest assured that Christ is also in *my* boat. He is my help in time of trouble. *'God is our refuge and strength, a very present help in trouble. Therefore we will not fear …'* (Ps. 46:1-2a ESV). He is Lord of the universe, and Lord of my life. Many challenges may feel too difficult for us to face, but nothing is beyond the power and grace of God. No challenge is too big for Him. He can bring peace out of the storm. He can bring new light and understanding about who He is. But we must be patient.

That is another lesson I am learning—patience. It took Jesus' disciples years to fully realize who they were in Christ, even though they were right by His side every single day. So, why should I think that Carl should fully understand who he is as a child of ours in a year or two? Does he understand more today than he did a year ago? Sure. He still has a long way to go, however, before he fully understands and embraces the joy of belonging, of brotherhood, of family. My prayer is that, through each and every storm that passes through our house, God will open up Carl's eyes just a little bit more to the secure reality of his status as a son. My prayer, too, is that God will open not only Carl's eyes, but also his ears, heart, and mind to the fact that Jesus is his Lord and Savior. Once Carl grasps that, then he will truly experience family, the family of God, for all eternity.

That snowy evening when Carl first ran away from home, God was faithful to answer our prayers. I had ventured up the street to the stop sign, calling out his name and keeping an eye open for any movement that might indicate his whereabouts. As I was about to turn to go down the intersecting street, I felt a pull inside of me to go back home. So I ran back to the house, expecting to find him there, but he had not returned. 'Lord, where is he? I need your help here. Please show me what to do.' That very instant, I began to think that I had never checked *behind* the house; I had only gone down the street in the front. When I ran to the back, I found Carl curled up in a little ball, under the table on our deck, shivering and crying. I sent a heartfelt thank-you up to God, and approached Carl slowly, not saying a word for fear that he would run again. I took my coat off and wrapped it around him, and motioned toward the back door. He would not look at me, but did agree to go inside. I so wanted to scoop him up in my arms to warm and comfort him, but he was not ready for that yet, so I simply walked with him up to his room, got him some socks for his frozen feet, and covered him with a blanket to help him warm up.

At this point, his crying had stopped, but he was still hurting. He initially crawled under his bed, and just laid there, not saying a word, but motioning for me to go away. I wanted him to see that I cared deeply for him and would always be there for him, no matter how good or difficult our days turn out to be. So, rather than leaving, I simply sat down on his floor and waited.

I'm not exactly sure what I was waiting *for*—maybe for the fear to subside in the heart of my boy, maybe for my own trepidations to melt away, maybe for him to warm up enough to stop shaking. Or, maybe I simply wanted to give him a tangible lesson in love. After 30 minutes or so, Carl did finally come out from under his bed, and crawled on top of it. He still was not making eye contact with me, but was noticeably more relaxed.

It was about this time that Jeff got home from work, and we both sat next to him on the bed, softly telling him how much we loved him, and how happy we were that God had brought him into our family. Our little dog even entered into that healing moment by jumping up next to Carl, and snuggling by his side.

Eventually, Carl rolled over, sat up, and hugged both his daddy and myself. I couldn't help but think that only God could bring such warmth and connection out of an evening that had initially been marked by fear and trembling. Yes, God is our help and our source of strength. He is our wisdom in times of trouble and uncertainty, and I praise Him for that. I am thankful, most of all, however, that God was kind enough to bring this incredible child into our home, for Carl's very presence here adds a new depth of care and love among us all. He is a precious gift to us, and I pray that one day he can see us as a gift to him as well. I realize this takes time, though; we are only at the beginning of a lifetime we will share together as a family.

Personal Reflections:

1. Read Psalm 66:5, 8, 10-12. Can you think of times in your life when you were tested, tried, burdened, overridden by others, or faced seemingly impossible situations? How did God draw you closer to Him during those times? In what ways did God nurture and mature you?

2. Read Romans 8:35, 38-39. Have you ever felt alone and unloved? How can these verses encourage you?

3. Read Mark 4:35-41. What are some ways this story can strengthen you when unexpected storms roll into your

life and the lives of your children? How can the reminder of who Christ is be our greatest source of strength?

4. Skim through the book of Mark and make a running record of who Christ is. Also, search out who you are as a follower of Christ. How can your understanding of these things be of importance to your life?

5. Read Psalm 46:1-2a. Ask God to search your heart and reveal to you the fears that may be affecting your life. How can the words of this passage bring peace in the midst of a fearful situation?

6. Write a prayer to God, praising Him for who He is. Be honest before Him with your worries and trepidations in life, and invite Him into these areas as your source of refuge and strength. Thank Him for specific ways He has shown Himself faithful to you in the past, and trust that He will continue to teach and mature you, strengthen you, and uplift you in the future.

3

Trust

Following the Example of Ananias

SOMETIMES I try to remember portions of my past, but the memories elude me, seeming to have vanished like morning mist. There are other moments in my life, however, that are inscribed so deeply in the crevices of my mind that even minute details of those experiences are not lost.

I'd like to share with you one of those more memorable days in my life. My husband had taken two of our children out of town, leaving me alone with our other three children. I remember waking up to a very wet, rainy Saturday morning. As the day progressed, the wind and rain picked up to the point that our power started flickering. There is a grocery store less than a mile down the street from our house, so I started thinking that we should run to the store to pick up some batteries for our flashlights just in case we were without power that night.

I herded the kids into the van, drove to the store, quickly ran in, grabbed a couple of sets of C batteries off the stand next to the register, then ran back to the van. In the short amount of time that I was in there, a storm came upon us like I had never experienced. I remember coming out of the store, and being stunned that it looked like it was nine o'clock at night, when, in reality, it was only three o'clock in the afternoon. The rain had picked up tremendously, and the wind was whipping all around us. I knew that home was just a few blocks down the street, so I hurried everyone into the van, and began a life-changing drive home.

As we pulled out of the parking lot, I could feel the wind press massively against the side of the van, and somewhere in the back of my mind, I recalled hearing on the radio earlier that morning that tornadoes had been spotted across North Carolina. I began to wonder if what we were experiencing was another tornado, or if my imagination was just getting the best of me. That question was quickly answered. After going just a few hundred yards down the street from the grocery store, things started to happen all around us: a giant, old oak tree fell across the road *behind* us, missing us by just inches, lightning struck about fifteen feet to the *right* of us, the roof of a small business on our *left* started coming off, smashing into our van, and directly in *front* of us, a huge SUV was picked up in the force of the swirling wind and turned so that it was facing the wrong way. My heart was racing as the reality of our situation quickly sunk in; we were, most certainly, in the middle of a tornado. I felt completely helpless and scared as I became keenly aware that life-threatening danger was looming around my three children and myself.

The winds were so strong at this point that I couldn't drive very fast, and the sheets of rain coming down were so thick that I couldn't see the road; for about fifteen seconds, it was literally as if someone had put an opaque white board in front of my windshield. All I could do was pray, asking God to help, protect and guide us, and something inside of me said to keep going … keep driving just a little bit farther down the road. If I could turn right into my neighborhood, and go down the hill, I would be able to see again. 'But Lord', I remember crying out, 'I am blind! I can't see where to turn; how can I do this?' And, in the midst of the storm, He said, 'Trust me.'

Trust in the Lord with all your heart, and do
not lean on your own understanding.
In all your ways acknowledge him, and he will
make straight your paths.
PROVERBS 3:5-6 (ESV)

Trust requires commitment and faith. To trust in some-
one is to rely on them, to believe in them. In Proverbs
chapter 3, we are promised that by trusting in the Lord
our paths will be made straight, that is to say, we will be
given direction for our lives.

(Bible Gateway, http://www.gospel.com/topics/trust+in
+the+lord+with+all+your+heart)

The Apostle Paul is an amazing person to study. Not because he was some 'super Christian,' but because he was a very real man who lived out his calling well. The first time we are introduced to Paul (known as Saul at that point), however, we are not given a picture of a man faithfully following Christ; rather, we are given a glimpse into the dark heart of a man with passionate desires against the purposes of God. Specifically, when Saul is initially written into the pages of Scripture, we see him as a murderer, approving the killing of Stephen, a believer in Christ.

> *Then they cast him (Stephen) out of the city and stoned him. And the witnesses laid down their garments at the feet of a young man named Saul.*
> ACTS 7:58 (ESV)

> *And Saul approved of his execution. And there arose on that day a great persecution against the church ...*
> ACTS 8:1 (ESV)

God did not desire for Saul to remain in this state of darkness, though, so on one very specific day, as Saul was traveling down a road leading to Damascus to further his mission to persecute Christians, Jesus engaged him in a life-changing encounter. This meeting would leave Saul physically blinded, but spiritually alive.

> *Now as he went on his way, he approached Damascus, and suddenly a light from heaven flashed around him. And falling to the ground he heard a voice saying to him, 'Saul, Saul, why are you persecuting me?' And he said, 'Who are you, Lord?' And he said, 'I am Jesus, whom you are persecuting.'*
> ACTS 9:3-5 (ESV)

As incredible as this part of the story is, I use it only as a springboard to usher us into the next section, where God speaks to another man, a disciple named Ananias. Even though Ananias lived in Damascus, and Saul lived in Jerusalem, news about the persecution and murders of Christians had spread like wildfire. This devout follower of Christ was well aware of the atrocities that were happening. So, can you imagine what must have been going through his mind when God commanded Ananias to go *to* Saul at a specified location in the city? Ananias had probably been pondering ways to stay in the shadows and remain as far *away* from Saul as possible! Let's read about it:

Now there was a disciple at Damascus named Ananias. The Lord said to him in a vision, 'Ananias.' And he said, 'Here I am, Lord.' And the Lord said to him, 'Rise and go to the street called Straight, and at the house of Judas look for a man of Tarsus named Saul, for behold, he is praying, and he has seen in a vision a man named Ananias come in and lay his hands on him so that he might regain his sight.' But Ananias answered, 'Lord, I have heard from many about this man, how much evil he has done to your saints at Jerusalem. And here he has authority from the chief priests to bind all who call on your name.' But the Lord said to him, 'Go, for he is a chosen instrument of mine to carry my name before the Gentiles and kings and the children of Israel. For I will show him how much he must suffer for the sake of my name.' So Ananias departed and entered the house. ...

Acts 9:10-17a

71

This passage opens in a most poignant way. God calls Ananias, and Ananias answers, *'Here I am, Lord.'* This response to God gives an immediate insight into the faith of this particular disciple, for his answer to God's call is one of recognition, eagerness, and respect. It reminds me of others in the Bible who responded similarly to God, such as Abraham (Gen. 22:1), Samuel (1 Sam. 3:10) and Isaiah (Isa. 6:8). Ananias heard and knew the voice of his Lord, and was eager to hear whatever good news God was bringing him that day. At least, that is how he felt until he actually heard the message: *'Rise and go … look for a man of Tarsus named Saul … and lay [your] hands on him so that he might regain his sight.'* I am sure that in that moment Ananias' heart went from being giddy with excitement, to trembling with fear. 'Lord, you must be talking about a different Saul. It can't be the one from Jerusalem who has been hunting down Christians, can it?' *'Lord, I have heard from many about this man, how much evil he has done to your saints at Jerusalem. And here he has authority from the chief priests to bind all who call on your name.'* 'Don't you get it, Lord? Saul could legally hurt me, imprison me, maybe even kill me! And you want me to go to him and help him? I'm not so sure about this.'

I have been thinking a lot lately about the inner turmoil Ananias must have felt during this conversation with God. He wanted to serve God and live out his calling, but he feared the unknown, the what-ifs, and the uncomfortable position he imagined this would put him in. For all Ananias knew, the act of obediently laying hands on Saul could very well have resulted in his own death. How do you resolve inner conflict like that? Even Jesus had asked God, regarding His upcoming crucifixion, *'Father, if you are willing, remove this cup from me'*

(Luke 22:42a ESV). I am certain that Ananias had a similar plea before the Father, desiring not to have this particular job assigned to him. I can't help but chuckle a little as Ananias pleads his case, reminding God of who Saul is (as if God had forgotten): *'Lord, I have heard from many about this man, how much evil he has done to your saints at Jerusalem. And here he has authority from the chief priests to bind all who call on your name.'* 'God,' I can hear him saying, 'have you forgotten how this man is going around and hurting your people? It seems to me that since he is now blind, you should leave him that way. What a blessing that would be! Why in the world do you want to help this evil man?'

Even after Ananias gets that off his chest, the Lord still says, *'Go.'* Yes, He adds a bit more, saying Saul is His chosen vessel and all, but He *doesn't* say, 'Ananias, I have grabbed hold of Saul's life and changed it for all time. He has been miraculously saved, and his heart now beats toward Me. The resurrected Jesus even had a conversation with Saul! So trust me that when you go to Saul, everything will be okay. You will not be harmed. In fact, you will be blessed.' No, God did not lay it out like that, so Ananias had to choose to *trust* God and move in the direction that God desired him to go, or he had to choose to turn *from* God and disobey this command out of the interest of self-preservation. Thankfully, he chose to follow the example Jesus had set before him, *'Nevertheless, not my will, but yours, be done'* (Luke 22:42b). We know this because he did not offer up any more objections to God, but simply obeyed, *'So Ananias departed and entered the house.'* There you have it. Even in his concern over what could happen to him if he approached Saul, Ananias chose to trust in God's character and limitless wisdom rather than relying on his own feelings and limited understanding.

Earlier in this chapter, I quoted Proverbs 3:5-6. It's such an important verse that I'd like to mention it again. *'Trust in the Lord with all your heart, and do not lean on your own understanding. In all your ways acknowledge him, and he will make straight your paths'* (ESV). Ananias chose to not lean on his own understanding of the situation with Saul; instead, he trusted that God would not ask him to do this deed if it didn't line up with His good will. He didn't need to know what the outcome would be, because he was confident in the character of God, and ultimately trusted Him with everything, even if that meant giving up his life to fulfill God's purposes.

Now, let's bring this story closer to home. Are there areas in your life where you feel overwhelmed? Or, do you feel called to do something, but uncertain about going down that path? Maybe God is telling you to find a counselor for your child, but you don't think any amount of talking could help. Maybe God is nudging you to reach out to someone to talk about your own personal struggles, but it's hard to believe that anyone could possibly understand what you are going through. Maybe God is opening your eyes to the fact that you need to change, when all you want is for your child to change. It could be any number of things, but we all have areas in our lives that we need to relinquish to God. Yet trusting others, even God, with the intricacies of our lives is not always easy, is it? It wasn't easy for Jesus to follow His call to go to the cross (even though He *did* trust God completely). It wasn't easy for Ananias to approach Saul. It wasn't easy for Abraham to place his son on an altar. It wasn't easy for Moses to make demands to the Pharaoh. So, don't be startled if the very thing God is calling you to do is difficult to walk through. Remember, just because something is hard does not mean that it is worthless, for God's plans always have great meaning to them.

We tend to go through life praying that our roads will not be full of speed bumps and pot holes, but God tells us up front that we can expect challenges, confrontations, and sufferings to arise. Don't be surprised by these things, and don't try so hard to avoid them. Rather, ask God to use you in the midst of them. When you adopt an older child, you cannot expect the process of integrating him into your family to be a bed of roses. The mere fact that this child was an orphan means that he experienced significant trauma in his life. God has called you to come alongside this child in his pain, fear, and frustration—to comfort him, help him, and give him a new foundation.

Every adoption looks different, and every child responds in a unique way to the joys and stresses of starting a new life. The first year after our adoption of Carl was difficult, to say the least. Our son was often afraid and lashed out with intense defensive actions. Responding to us in the only ways he knew how, he spat on people, bullied his brother, ran away from home, called me horrid names, and, in many ways, acted like an out-of-control three year old, even though he was twelve. He didn't know any better, though, for the foundation of a stable family unit had been missing from his life. Even though I was aware of that in the abstract, my world was rocked to the core when I saw these realities lived out, and I found myself caught in the middle of a difficult life, not knowing how to parent Carl and help him heal from past abuses, not knowing how to control my own poor responses to his actions, not knowing how best to help my spouse and other children navigate these changes, and not knowing where to go for help.

Over and over in his letters, though, Paul tells us that Christ is the answer and hope to every problem. He is the …

Creator,

Sustainer,

Healer,

Savior,

Comforter,

Giver of gifts,

Sovereign Lord,

and He is greater than any challenge we will ever face. We must, therefore, be willing to step back from the tunnel-visioned view of our circumstances so that we can see that there is a future in store for us and our children, and humbly look to Christ for a new perspective on that life—*His* perspective. We must search Scripture and remind ourselves what Christ has done for us, allowing our actions to flow from that truth. Is that easy to do? No, not really. I have to admit that when I was in the middle of my most difficult days with Carl, I wanted a number of 'me-centered' things, such as respect from Carl (even though he had no idea what respect looked like). I wanted others to see how difficult my situation was and feel sorry for me, and on some days, I wanted most of all for the traumatic events to end, and for life to resume at a 'normal' pace. I was focusing on me and my selfish desires, so it took me a long time to hear God's voice in all this, His whispers of hope being offered to me. Once I did, though, everything began to change.

I thought that after a year or so Carl would be well adjusted and happily fitting into his new family. In some ways that was true, but in other ways that was anything but true. I could not understand why the simplest thing would set him off so quickly and so strongly that he would be in a tirade for two hours or so before he would calm down enough for us to talk to him. I had never in my life had anyone yell at me like he did, much less call me awful names that made me cringe, and I found that I responded to his anger with my own anger. I demanded that he respect me. I demanded that he follow the rules. And I demanded that he respect others. I was wrong in demanding like that, but I wanted him to learn on my terms, and respond to me like his siblings did. I couldn't understand why that was so hard for him to do. (Unfortunately, for a season, I had forgotten the grace that Christ had extended to me when I was lost and rebellious). Then, there were days when all I could do was to hold Carl tight while he was screaming, telling him that we love him. There were other days when I had to rally neighbors to help me look for Carl because he had run away. And there was even a day when, for the first time, I had to dig deep within myself to humbly ask God where I was going wrong, after my son hit me strongly across the face during one of his episodes.

That night, after my husband came home, he saw the bloody mark across my cheek, and I just broke down and cried in his arms. 'What are we doing? I know for sure that God brought Carl into our home, but how are we supposed to raise him? He has experienced twelve years of abandonment and abuse, so whenever I need to correct him on anything, his mind immediately switches to survival mode. He told me that when he was in the orphanage, whenever he would make the smallest mistake, one of his caretakers would do things like yell at him, hit him, whip him, or slam his head into a concrete wall to discipline him. Carl has been here a year, and he still fights the fear that I am going to do something just as horrid to him. I don't know what to do anymore. I am so tired and weary. I had no idea it was going to be this hard.'

To that, my husband, Jeff, answered that we need to ask God to forgive us for thinking we could help Carl on our own, and ask Him to give us wisdom on what to do from here on out. He said that it was important for us to keep being there for Carl, teaching him the gospel of Christ. As important as rules and respect are for the functioning of a household, we had to remind ourselves that no amount of rules would actually heal the brokenness that Carl is feeling inside; only the love, power, and mercy of God Almighty can reach into his heart and heal what has been damaged. As we talked, it became crystal clear that by bringing Carl into our home, God had planted us right in the middle of a mission field, and that we had to keep moving forward with *Christ* as our head, our wisdom, and our strength. Then Jeff reminded me that no one ever said that living out our callings in life was going to be easy. In fact, Paul tells us not only to expect hard times and suffering, but that we are to *'declare … the gospel of God in the midst of conflict'* (1 Thess. 2:2b ESV).

Looking at difficult circumstances of life from a Christ-centric point of view changes everything. No longer do I have to rely on my own wisdom to be an effective parent, but rather, I am learning to prayerfully lean into Jesus, and to yield to His plans and purposes daily, even moment-by-moment. I am not, however, perfect in this trust, for Carl can be very strong, forceful, and violent, and I can be quite self-centered and egotistical.

I do find, however, that I can draw strength and courage from the God-breathed words of Scripture. For instance, we can learn much from Paul and how he handled difficult situations he faced in life. Paul teaches us by example that we should not pray for our chains to go away, or that our circumstances should get better, or that we could live in ease, but that we may be worthy witnesses no matter where we are in life. He encourages us to share with all (including our children) what the Lord has done for us. He exhorts us to courageously keep going down the paths we are called to, remembering constantly that even those situations that are extremely difficult to handle and live through are not beyond the reach of God's grace. The more God matures us and draws us closer in relationship with Christ, the more our hearts desperately want to trust Him, cling to Him, and hear and recognize His voice, and experience His peace, even in the midst of a storm. With that trust, guidance, and peace, the Holy Spirit enables us to imitate the way Paul gently led people. If Paul was hurt or disrespected, he did not retaliate or demand respect, but rather, he went to the Lord in prayer and reflected on who he was in Christ, a broken, sinful man who had been given the amazing free gift of forgiveness and salvation. This gave him the ability to love, lead, and forgive even when he was hurt, because he, himself, had already been forgiven.

Later in the day, after the incident when Carl hit me, after he had had some time to cool down, I had a chance to talk to him. He looked tenderly at the redness on my cheek, and asked me to forgive him for hurting me. That was the perfect opportunity to gently explain to him that in my lifetime, I had repeatedly hurt and disrespected Christ, yet He always forgave me for those wrongs. Because of that, I explained, I was able to truly forgive Carl for hurting me, too. As we hugged, I could sense one small chunk of Carl's protective wall coming down. I prayed that God would continue to use me and the rest of the family to show Carl, in very real, concrete ways, what the gospel was all about, and that God would draw Carl lovingly to Himself. Yes, at times it is physically and emotionally draining to live out this calling, but I keep Galatians 6:9 posted on my bathroom mirror to remind me to keep going, even when I feel like giving up. It says, *'And let us not grow weary of doing good, for in due season we will reap a harvest, if we do not give up'.*

Do not give up! Do not lose hope! Sometimes it is difficult to do the things we are called to do because our emotions deceive us, tempting us to believe that the hard days will never end, that we are incapable of change, and that we are wasting our time, perhaps even harming the rest of our family in the process. Instead, we must look beyond our present situations, keep our eyes above the horizon, and hang onto the hope we have in Christ. 1 John 3:16-18 says:

This is how we know what love is: Jesus Christ laid down his life for us. And we ought to lay down our lives for our brothers. If anyone has material possessions and sees his brother in need but has no pity on him, how can the love of God be in him? Dear children, let us not love with words or tongue but with actions and in truth.

No one ever said that adoption would be easy. It may be wonderful, and well worth the effort (I definitely think so!), but it is not easy. In fact, we have found that it is one of the most selfless things a person can do, for it involves giving your life to another (John 15:13). Because of that, I am reminded daily of the fact that Christ gave His life for us. He didn't do it because we were perfect, kind, or lovely. He did it because *He* is perfect, kind and lovely, and He desired to extend His grace to us so that we could be brought into relationship with Him. Likewise, we must never lose sight of the fact that our children have been given to us so that we can care for them, even when they are difficult; so we can love them, even when they rebel; and so we can give our lives to them, even when they are not appreciative.

Do you see that in the very act of selflessly giving your life to bring up and nurture your children, you are giving them a glimpse into the character of God? Your love for them is not conditional. It will never end. It is a love that goes beyond expectations, and is life-giving, no matter the cost. The Hebrew word for this type of love is *hesed*, and is perfectly seen in the love God graciously gives to His children. It is the *'consistent, ever-faithful, relentless, constantly-pursuing, lavish, extravagant, unrestrained, furious love of our Father God!'* (http://www. hesed.com/hesed.html). God's *hesed* for us is sacrificial, has no bounds, and is all-encompassing, for all time. It is a love that we can cling to, a love that will not fail us, a love we can trust.

TRUST:
1. Assured reliance on the character, ability, strength, or truth of someone or something

2. One in which confidence is placed
    (http://www.merriam-webster.com/dictionary/trust)

Our trust in God is not simply an empty hope or a wishful thought, but a very real, grounded belief that God is who He says He is. When I think of complete trust, an image of my two youngest daughters comes to mind. Most mornings, right before Jeff goes off to work, these girls yell, 'Jump hug, Daddy!!' They run up about six or seven steps while their daddy stands at the bottom with outstretched arms. Then, one at a time, each girl counts 1-2-3, and then jumps with no reservation or fear right into the capable arms of their father, who always catches them. I would like to encourage you to fill yourself up with the truths of Scripture so that when the hard days come (and they will come!), you will be prepared to jump securely into the arms of your heavenly Father, with no hesitancy because you are sure He will catch you. As you read through the Bible, you will find a myriad of God's attributes—truths you can hold to when you need them the most. To get you started on this quest to learn more about God and His character, consider this short passage from Exodus 34:5-6, where God further discloses to Moses who He is:

> *Then the LORD came down in the cloud and stood there with him and proclaimed his name, the LORD. And he passed in front of Moses, proclaiming, 'The LORD, the LORD, the compassionate and gracious God, slow to anger, abounding in love and faithfulness …'.*

Let's look at each of these traits one at a time, comparing them with other Scriptures, to give us a deeper understanding of who our God is. As you walk through the joys and trials of your life, ask the Holy Spirit to make clear to you which verse(s) or divine character traits He would have you cling to in that moment.

THE LORD

◆ **PSALM 54:4**
Surely God is my help; the Lord is the One who sustains me.

◆ **PSALM 147:5**
Great is our Lord and mighty in power; his understanding has no limit.

◆ **2 SAMUEL 22:2-3**
The LORD is my rock, my fortress and my deliverer;
my God is my rock, in whom I take refuge,
my shield and the horn of my salvation.
He is my stronghold, my refuge and my Savior …

◆ **NEHEMIAH 4:14**
After I looked things over, I stood up and said to the nobles, the officials and the rest of the people, 'Don't be afraid of them. Remember the LORD, who is great and awesome, and fight for your families, your sons and your daughters, your wives and your homes.'

◆ **GENESIS 18:14a**
Is anything too hard for the LORD?

◆ **PSALM 145:18**
The LORD is near to all who call on him, to all who call on him in truth.

COMPASSIONATE

◆ **PSALM** 145:9

The LORD is good to all; he has compassion on all he has made.

◆ **PSALM** 103:13

As a father has compassion on his children, so the LORD has compassion on those who fear him.

◆ **ISAIAH 49:13**

Shout for joy, you heavens;
rejoice, you earth;
burst into song, you mountains!
For the LORD comforts his people
and will have compassion on his afflicted ones.

◆ **JAMES 5:11**

As you know, we count as blessed those who have persevered. You have heard of Job's perseverance and have seen what the Lord finally brought about. The Lord is full of compassion and mercy.

GRACIOUS

◆ **ISAIAH 30:18a**

Yet the LORD longs to be gracious to you;
therefore he will rise up to show you compassion.

◆ **2 CORINTHIANS 9:8**

And God is able to make all grace abound to you, so that having all sufficiency in all things at all times, you may abound in every good work (ESV).

◆ **2 CORINTHIANS 12:9**

But he said to me, 'My grace is sufficient for you, for my power is made perfect in weakness.' Therefore, I will boast all the more gladly about my weaknesses, so that Christ's power may rest on me.

◆ **HEBREWS 4:16**
Let us then approach God's throne of grace with confidence, so that we may receive mercy and find grace to help us in our time of need.

SLOW TO ANGER

◆ **NUMBERS 14:18a**
The LORD is slow to anger, abounding in love and forgiving sin and rebellion.

◆ **NEHEMIAH 9:17b**
… But you are a forgiving God, gracious and compassionate, slow to anger and abounding in love. Therefore you did not desert them…

◆ **JOEL 2:13**
Rend your heart and not your garments. Return to the LORD your God, for he is gracious and compassionate, slow to anger and abounding in love, and he relents from sending calamity.

◆ **NAHUM 1:3a**
The LORD is slow to anger but great in power…

ABOUNDING IN LOVE

◆ **PSALM 62:11-12a**
Once God has spoken;
twice have I heard this:
that power belongs to God,
and that to you, O Lord, belongs steadfast love (ESV).

- **PSALM** 107:8-9

  Let them thank the LORD for his steadfast love,
  for his wondrous works to the children of man!
  For he satisfies the longing soul,
  and the hungry soul he fills with good things (ESV).

- **PSALM** 86:5

  You, LORD, are forgiving and good, abounding in love to
  all who call to you.

- **PSALM** 100:5

  For the LORD is good and his love endures forever;
  his faithfulness continues through all generations.

ABOUNDING IN FAITHFULNESS

- **DEUTERONOMY 31:6**

  Be strong and courageous. Do not be afraid or terrified
  because of them, for the LORD your God goes with you;
  he will never leave you nor forsake you.

- **PSALM** 9:10

  Those who know your name trust in you,
  for you, LORD, have never forsaken those who seek you.

- **PSALM** 145:13b-14

  The LORD is trustworthy in all he promises
  and faithful in all he does.
  The LORD upholds all who fall
  and lifts up all who are bowed down.

- **PSALM** 89:8

  Who is like you, LORD God almighty?
  You, LORD, are mighty, and your faithfulness surrounds
  you.

Remember the tornado that I spoke about at the beginning of this chapter, in which my children and I were caught? Well, we did choose to trust God and His leading. Not being able to see the road at all due to the horrific sheet of rain, I blindly turned where I felt God said to turn, and, indeed, we stayed on the road, rather than ending up in a ditch. Immediately, as we descended the hill into our neighborhood, the storm began to wane, and my visibility came back. We quickly drove to our house, stunned by the damage all around us, for we saw roofs torn off neighbors' homes, cars thrown around as if they were toys, and even some houses that were completely flattened. Our home was still standing, though, so we ran inside, grabbed our two little dogs, and took refuge in the downstairs bathroom. In there we huddled together and cried out to God, asking Him for His protection. I remember my two biological children praying out loud with me, when my eleven-year-old son, Jeffery, stopped, and looked at our newly adopted son, Carl. The notion of God was fairly new for Carl, and he was still struggling with the idea that God is real, so he just sat there, waiting for the storm to pass. In that raw moment, God used Jeffery to try to help Carl see our need for God. Jeffery tenderly said, 'Carl, come pray with us. God is bigger than this storm, and He is the only one who can bring us through it. Come pray, Carl, pray!' We couldn't do one single thing to save ourselves at that moment … it all rested completely in His hands. But His hands are good, loving hands, and we could trust Him with everything. In essence, Jeffery was pleading for Carl to join hands with us, and see just how great our God is. And with that, God began to further open Carl's heart and mind.

We knew that day that whether we lived or died was in the hands of our heavenly Father. We knew that the very breath we breathed was due to His sustenance. And in that moment, our deepest prayer was that we would be held by the One who created everything, by the One who holds it all together, by the One who loved us enough to allow us to live through this intense experience so that we could be drawn closer to Him in faith, trust, and love. As the storm swirled all around us, we began to sit peacefully in our home, glorifying God, awestruck by His power and majesty; and we asked Him to help us to remember to be this dependent on Him not just when life was hard, but in every moment of every day.

Personal Reflections:

1. Read Proverbs 3:5-8. These verses are all about trust. Are there areas in your life right now that you are trying to fix or control in your own power? What does it say in verse 8 about trusting in God? How can this happen when you are in the middle of one of life's storms? What keeps you from trusting God in moments of peril or difficulty?

2. Read Psalm 139:23-24. Ask God to search your heart and reveal to you places that are in rebellion against Him and His plans for your life. You may not even be aware of these sins, but God is, and He delights in helping you to change so that you can walk closer to Him.

3. Read 2 Corinthians 10:3-6. These verses contain powerful words, educating and reminding us of the reality of spiritual warfare. Satan will try to bring us down and pit family members against each other. Understand the importance of fighting these battles with the knowledge and wisdom God

gives us through Scripture. 'Take every thought captive' toward Christ so that you don't become mentally defeated by the weaknesses of your own fallen mind.

4. Read back through the Scriptures mentioned earlier in this chapter that illuminate various attributes of God. The Lord is compassionate … gracious … slow to anger … abounding in love … abounding in faithfulness. Which ones speak to your life today? Which ones bring healing, hope, strength, refreshment and/or peace to you? Write those down on a note card and keep them some place where you will see them often. Memorize them, and trust the Holy Spirit to bring them to mind when you need them the most.

4

Gaining Perspective

Noticing God's Chariots in Our Lives

IT was the Fourth of July, and our neighborhood was having a pool party to celebrate. We had four children at the time, and they were all thrilled to take part in the festivities. Evidently, we were not the only ones eager to celebrate that day, for the pool was crawling with families.

Our children were young then, ages one, three, five and seven. I remember laughing as my three-year-old daughter, Felicia, was trying to out-do her seven-year-old sister, Abigail, in the hula hoop competition. Of course, Abigail was much more skilled in the activity, so Felicia finally settled for just looking cute. She was already showing the instincts of a fashion designer, so she picked out a lemon-yellow hula hoop that looked great with her bright lime-green swim suit. I can still see her posing for pictures.

After hula hooping, Abigail jumped back into the pool to swim some more, and my five-year-old, Jeffery, and I went to the far side of the pool, to the only lounge chair that was open, to rest and have a snack. Meanwhile, my husband, Jeff, took our two youngest daughters, Madison and Felicia, to the restroom. I recall watching those two little ones walking away from the pool, and Felicia taking off her life jacket, preparing ahead of time to 'go potty.' While waiting for their return, I chatted with Jeffery as we shared a snack of grapes. Moments later, I noticed Jeff and the two girls returning from the restroom, heading back to the pool. What I didn't notice, though, was Madison, my baby, turning and running back into the bathroom, and my husband going after her. Evidently, Felicia didn't realize that her daddy was no longer right by her side, so she must have jumped into the pool, believing either her daddy would jump in after her, or thinking her life-vest would keep her afloat. Unfortunately, though, her daddy was running after her sister, and Felicia had forgotten to put her life-vest back on.

Our pool is fairly small, but, as I said before, it was packed with families having a great time. There must have been about one hundred people there! Even with the water teeming with people, as soon as I looked back at the pool, my eyes immediately focused on something under the water, something lime-green under the surface. My heart stopped, as I knew that was Felicia.

For the next little bit of time, it was as if everything moved in slow motion. I screamed Felicia's name, but, of course, she couldn't hear me. So I yelled to Abigail, who was not far from Felicia, to help her little sister. There were so many people talking, however, that she could see me trying to tell her something, but couldn't make out the words. I was all tangled up in towels, and had snacks and my son on my lap, so it seemed like an eternity before I could break loose. There I was, on the opposite end of the pool from where my little girl was desperately trying to survive, and I just couldn't seem to get to her. There were so many people there, so why didn't anyone notice her struggling? Why couldn't anyone hear my screams?

Finally, *finally*, I got to her, just as her head came up out of the water. Somehow she had gotten herself close enough to the steps so that she could get out. She was crying, coughing, and asking where I had been when she was so scared. My heart soared with the realization that she was alive, but it also hurt dreadfully, as I began to ponder my helplessness in the whole situation.

That night I remember playing and replaying, over and over in my mind, the events from that day, and I could feel myself becoming depressed. 'Lord, you called me to be a mother, but I can't do it. It's too hard for me, and lives are at stake. Why did I ever think that I should have so many kids? Oh, Lord, we made a mistake. I feel so paralyzed in parenting right now. I can't do this anymore. It's too much responsibility, and I have proven today that parenting well is beyond me.' My thoughts swirled around these worries as I drifted off to a fitful sleep that night.

Out of the depths I cry to you, O Lord!
O Lord, hear my voice!
Let your ears be attentive
to the voice of my pleas for mercy!

I wait for the Lord, my soul waits,
and in his word I hope;
my soul waits for the Lord
more than watchmen for the morning,

more than watchmen for the morning.
O Israel, hope in the Lord!
For with the Lord there is steadfast love,
and with him is plentiful redemption.
PSALM 130:1-2, 5-7 (ESV)

Sometimes I come across verses in the Bible that calm and warm my fearful heart in ways that only a genuine, close friend can do. After the experience with my daughter at the pool, I cried out to God, shaken and fearful. The reality of just how weak and fallible I was hit me like a punch to my stomach, and I found myself being quickly pulled into a mire of anxiety. Logically, I knew that God had miraculously saved Felicia from death that day, and I wanted to celebrate, but I couldn't pull myself away from what my heart had felt during those moments of intense adrenaline and dread. '*Out of the depths I cry to you, O Lord! O Lord, hear my voice! Let your ears be attentive to the voice of my pleas for mercy!'* 'Forgive me, Lord, for not keeping an eye on Felicia when she came out of the restroom, and forgive me for doubting your presence and ability to help her.'

Many days I have fallen into similar fears regarding Carl. 'Forgive me, Lord, for sometimes wondering if my son had it in him to truly love others, for I was wrong. Forgive me, Lord, for doubting at times Your involvement in his life, for You are there. Forgive me, Lord, for becoming anxious about his healing quickly from his past trauma, for some things just take time.' At various points in my life, my faith has faltered, and my emotions have hung on what I can see and feel rather than on what I believe and hope for. Thankfully, God accepts me and loves me, even when I pour out my tumultuous heart to him. I cannot hide before God, for He knows my inmost being. I cannot lie to God about how I feel, for He is Truth, and untruth cannot stand before Him. No, I find that when I lay myself before the Lord, and openly admit my worries to Him, He quietly listens with grace and understanding, and often stirs my heart with reminders that I need to hear: 'Thank you for coming to Me with your cries for mercy. With Me, you will find answers. You will find peace. I will never leave you nor forsake you. Put it all out there. Get it off your chest, and lay it on Mine, for I can carry those heavy burdens that you were never meant to take on. Carl is Mine, and his healing rests in My hands, not yours. His heart will change only when I touch it, and not before. That is not what you ought to worry about. That is not your calling. I have called you to love him, to parent him, and, most importantly, to teach him about Me. I am at work in his life. Even when it seems as if years are passing by without the changes you are hoping for, keep moving forward, for I am working in ways that may not be readily apparent for a long time.'

Let us not become weary in doing good, for at the proper time we will reap a harvest if we do not give up.
GALATIANS 6:9

On my worst days, when I am irritable and tired, I tend to take my pity party to God while wearing dark, self-centered glasses. At those moments, I am only able to see the dire circumstances right in front of me, rather than God's glorious plan being worked out all around me. As I focus on Scripture, however, the Holy Spirit begins to lift my chin so that I can see beyond the moment. He fills me with hope for a future for Carl, and changes my anxiety into expectation. God's Word, as I've discovered time and time again, is living and active, and speaks life like nothing else can. That's not to say that I am given all the answers every time I read the Bible, but I *am* given an assurance that the Lord is with us, and that makes all the difference. '*I wait for the Lord, my soul waits, and in his word I hope; my soul waits for the Lord more than watchmen for the morning, more than watchmen for the morning. O Israel, hope in the Lord!*' As God adjusts my view to see with eyes of faith, I begin to understand that His hand is moving in all things. Subsequently, my ability to wait patiently grows as He continues to work in Carl's life. As my heart steadies, and my perspective centers on Christ, I am able to praise Him and glorify Him, even when I do not yet see the answers for which I am longing.

'*My soul waits for the Lord more than watchmen for the morning.*' Think about that poetic statement for a moment. What does a watchman do? He keeps a vigilant lookout for the enemy, knowing that in the depths of the darkness surrounding him, conditions are favorable for an attack. When we are at our lowest, struggling daily with intense parenting conditions, we must be aware that the devil may step in during those raw, vulnerable moments in an attempt to pull us down. He would like nothing more than to see us give up on our calling, on our child, on God. Satan seeks to steal, kill and destroy (John 10:10), and he will attack from unexpected directions in an effort to steal our hope and joy, kill our relationships, and destroy our families.

God, however, is mightier than Satan ever will be. We must remember that Christ was triumphant over Satan two thousand years ago when He willingly gave His life for us on the cross, and rose victoriously from the grave. Christ won the battle! Praise God! Do you realize that the power that worked in Christ to raise Him from the dead is the exact same power working in your life if you are one of His children? Do not underestimate that power. Rather, hang onto it, believing that even if you are in the midst of dark troubles, and cannot see the light ahead, God will give you the strength to keep moving forward, believing that He is, indeed, working out His plan for you and your children. The night may be longer, darker, and colder than you ever expected, but, just as the watchmen knew that the morning would eventually arrive, hang on diligently to the hope that you have in God for a brilliant future. God is certainly near. The more you understand the presence of God in your life situation, the more you will experience the peace that can only come from Him.

> *I bless the Lord who gives me counsel;*
> *in the night also my heart instructs me.*
> *I have set the Lord always before me;*
> *because he is at my right hand, I shall not be shaken.*
> PSALM 16:7-8 (ESV)

Quite often, hope comes when we least expect it, when we are at our lowest points—when it looks like there is no way out, and that we are trapped in the circumstances of life. I found this to be true in a marvelous story in 2 Kings 6:8-17. More than once, the message in this chapter has encouraged me to keep moving forward; for even when I feel alone and afraid,

I am reminded of the fact that the Lord is with me, and with God in my corner, we have the advantage.

This scene opens with a frustrated Syrian king. He had tried numerous times to attack Israel, but his plans were continually thwarted. Somehow, the Israelite king was learning of the Syrian king's battle plans, and thus was able to avoid being overtaken. The king of Syria began to think that someone from his own kingdom was betraying him by passing on his plans of attack to the king of Israel: *'Will you not show me who of us is for the king of Israel?'* (v. 11 ESV).

One of his servants assured him that none of them had done such a thing, but that a man of God, a prophet, was given wisdom as to the plans of the Syrian king. *'... Elisha, the prophet who is in Israel, tells the king of Israel the words that you speak ...'* (v. 12 ESV). Alarmed at this man's ability to know the military plans of the enemy even before they are acted upon, the Syrian king then set out to capture Elisha so that he could no longer deliver this privy information to the king of Israel. With this goal in mind, a plan was devised that involved a clandestine attack on Elisha. *'So he sent there horses and chariots and a great army, and they came by night and surrounded the city'* (v. 14 ESV). This was an all-out stealth move, where large numbers of military men were employed to surround this man of God while he was sleeping, with the intent of overpowering him in the morning. The king must have been certain that Elisha had no way out, and that this would be a quick maneuver. He was probably thinking that they would go in, take hold of Elisha at daybreak, bring him back to the Syrian camp, and then turn right around to attack the king of Israel. God, however, had other plans.

The first person to get up and walk outside that fateful morning after the Syrian army poised itself for attack was not

Elisha, but his servant. *'When the servant of the man of God rose early in the morning and went out, behold, an army with horses and chariots was all around the city. And the servant said, "Alas, my master! What shall we do?"'* (v. 15). In this story, I wish I could say that I could relate most to the prophet Elisha, but my experiences are more in tune with this servant. He woke up that morning expecting to go through the normal routines of the day, when, all of a sudden, he was caught up in frightening circumstances that were unexpected and beyond his control. I can picture him stepping outside as he was yawning and stretching, still waking up, when something caught his eye. It was not one or two men with swords that grabbed his attention, but an entire army, complete with state-of-the-art chariots! Immediately, his senses must have gone into high alert, his knees probably started shaking, and his heart, I am sure, began to feel that sense of impending doom.

I can relate. There have been numerous days when I was going about the normal routines of my day and a situation arose in the house, causing Carl to go into his intense place of either fear, fight, or flight. Whenever this has happened, I felt just like Elisha's servant: all my senses sharpened as I prepared to face the battle before me, my hands literally shook from the anxiety of not knowing what was going to happen, and my heart dropped as I dreaded the intense confrontation that I was inevitably about to face.

After the servant's fearful comment was made, in which he wondered what they should do, Elisha reassured him with some amazing words. First, he said, *'Do not be afraid'* (v. 16). What? Did you say to not be afraid? I can just hear his servant now responding with something like, 'Elisha, are you still asleep? Open your eyes. I know it's still kind of dark out here, but look around you. We are completely surrounded by well-armed people who obviously want to overtake us. Any moment now they are going to charge at us. We are doomed. Sitting ducks, with no way out. What do you mean, don't be afraid?!'

'Do not be afraid.' That statement reminds me of Jesus in the midst of the storm. His disciples were frantic with fear, but Jesus was sleeping, because He knew that He was greater than the storm, and that He had perfect command over the circumstances and the outcome of that day. As Jesus calmed the winds and sea with His words, those with Him began to see a bit clearer how they never needed to fear, for the Lord of lords was right there in the boat with them all along (Mark 4:35-41).

In a similar fashion, Elisha helped his servant to see the reality of the situation around them. Yes, it was a fact that they were surrounded by warriors who had the intent to capture them, to silence the messenger of God, to overcome this good with evil. As always, Satan thinks that he can outsmart God and prevent his plans from coming to fruition. At times, the devil surrounds us with confusion and seemingly impossible circumstances, and whispers into our ears that we are outnumbered, defeated. He wants us to believe that nothing can change the heart of the child that we adopted, that there will always be conflict in our home and despair in their lives. He wants us to think that we are ill equipped for the job of raising our child, and cannot effectively parent him. He wants us to believe that our child isn't going to grow and change, and that he is unreachable. Ultimately, Satan wants us to think that we made a mistake, and that we cannot make a difference.

Lies. Those words are all lies. They sound so real, however, because they feed on our fears. But they originate with a habitual liar. John 8:44b tells us these words about Satan: '*He was a murderer from the beginning, not holding to the truth, for there is not truth in him. When he lies, he speaks his native language, for he is a liar and the father of lies.'* John 10:10a says, *'the thief (Satan) comes only to steal and kill and destroy'* (ESV). Satan does not want our families to thrive; he wants to break them apart. If we lose hope in the one true God, as well as hope in the life of our troubled children, then that gives a foothold to the devil. Don't lose hope! Hang onto it with everything you have, for it is good and true and the reality that God wants us to see. Where Satan comes to kill, steal, and destroy, Jesus tells a contrasting reality about Himself. Listen to the rest of that verse: *'The thief (Satan) comes only to steal and kill and destroy. I (Jesus) came that they may have life and have it abundantly'* (ESV). Jesus brings life, not destruction.

See the wisdom in Elisha's instructing his servant to not fear. He goes on to teach and comfort this man who is shaking in his boots by telling him, *'... those who are with us are more than those who are with them'* (2 Kings 6:16b). One of the many things that I love about our God is that He truly cares for us. He knows that we need Him in life, so He never leaves our side. He created us to need each other, too, so it is no wonder that God used Elisha to uplift and encourage the servant in his hour of need. God had given Elisha the gift of being able to see into the spiritual realm, and, in an effort to help his servant let go of his fear, Elisha asked the Lord to open his servant's eyes as well to the spiritual reality surrounding them. *'Then Elisha prayed and said, "O Lord, please open his eyes that he may see." So the Lord opened the eyes of the young man, and he saw, and behold, the mountain was full of horses and chariots of fire all around Elisha'* (2 Kings 6:17). God's army had been in position all along, surrounding the enemy, outnumbering the Syrian army, protecting the men of God. In his inability to see God's army, however, the servant thought he was facing impossible odds alone. He and Elisha were never alone, though, were they? What an incredible eye-opener that must have been! I think if I had been the servant at that moment, realizing with great clarity that I was going to be okay after all, I would have crumpled to the ground with cries of relief and gratitude. The Lord's army was exceedingly powerful, and ready to protect them, ready to do battle against the enemy, ready to win.

Sometimes God gives us, the parents, a new, fresh perspective on a situation to help us carry on. Other times, he opens the eyes of our children in unanticipated ways, aiding them in their journey of healing while they acclimatize to their new families. One afternoon, my children and I were upstairs, enjoying some time together, playing a board game. Games have always been an integral part of our family, and tend to draw us closer together. On this particular day, however, something selfish was said by one of my younger children that set Carl off into a world of rage. A tiny trigger caused something in his mind to shift to a place of defense. I did not handle the situation very well that day, and spoke to him harshly out of my frustration. Of course, that only proved to accelerate his anger, and he stormed out of the room, upset, fearful, and out of control. As he ran downstairs, he screamed that he was going to run away, that our family stank, and that he never wanted to see us again. My heart was racing as I heard the front door slam shut.

I have never gotten used to how quickly storms like that can arise. They shake me up every time, for I love Carl, and desperately want him to know that, even though I can't seem to get through to him sometimes. This wasn't the first time Carl had threatened to run away, and I had learned from experience that he never went far. I wanted to run after him, to calm his fears, and to bring him back, but I had also learned that going after him right away would prove to be useless. He needed time to calm down a bit before we could approach him. So, as we stood there, I gathered together my other children, had us hold hands in a circle, and began to pray for Carl. I didn't know what else to do.

'Lord, I love You, and am thankful that You are with us, right here in the middle of our troubles. You never get so disgusted or frustrated with us that You leave. Thank You for that, because we need You right now. Lord, would You please forgive me for raising my voice to Carl when I should have stayed calm? I am so sorry. I keep messing up in that way, and I know that I need to change. On my own power, though, I can't seem to shake how I react to Carl when he escalates and gets angry. I need You. Would You please change my heart, Lord? Help me to understand Carl's actions better so that I can be the parent he needs me to be.

'And, Lord, we ask that You look after Carl right now. I don't know where he has gone, but I know that You know exactly where he is. Please calm his heart and cover him with Your warm arms of love and peace. Speak to him, Lord, and let him know that he is loved deeply, and that he belongs in this family. Give him an assurance, Lord, that he is secure here, and that there is nothing he can do that will ever make us send him away. We love him so much, Lord. Please open up his eyes to see that. Thank You. In Jesus' holy name, amen.'

As we finished the prayer, feeling calmer and more assured of God's presence in the situation at hand, we started to head downstairs to go find Carl and bring him home. As I turned the corner to go down the steps, I was surprised to find Carl standing on the landing at the bottom. He was looking up at me with big eyes, and his body language told me that he was calm and peaceful. As I slowly descended the stairs, heading toward him, he began to talk: 'Mom, a few minutes ago when I ran out of the room, I pretended like I was going outside. I was angry at you and wanted to hear what you said about me when you thought I wasn't around. I thought for sure you would say bad things about me, like how I make your life hard, and how you wish I wasn't even there. But that's not what you said at all. Instead of talking junk about me, you prayed for me. I didn't expect that. You actually do love me, don't you?'

What a beautiful day that was, as I could see God working in the middle of the turmoil in our home. Immediately, I could see why the Holy Spirit impressed on my heart so strongly to stop for a moment to pray before going out to look for my son. He knew that Carl was in listening-distance, and that he needed to hear those tender words of love. That was not my doing, but God's, as He orchestrated His plan through us. It's quite wonderful how God chose to use something normal in our home—a time of prayer—to reach Carl that day. It completely diffused his anger and changed his perspective on how we felt about him. In the matter of about two minutes, God gave our son a glimpse into the reality that he is not alone in this world, but has a place where he belongs, a place where he is genuinely loved.

As you venture down the paths of parenthood, I encourage you to trust that God is working, bringing about His plans and purposes for you and your family. I realize that some days will appear to be more than you can handle, and there will be moments when you feel outnumbered, weak, and all alone. On those days, take captive your thoughts, and hang on to the glorious hope that is found in Christ Jesus.

> *Do not be afraid.*
> *Do not lose hope.*
> *Do not allow yourself to believe that your*
>   *situation is too great for the Lord to handle.*

Take your eyes off what you see here on earth for a moment, and ask God to show you that there is a heavenly reality surrounding your situation. God has a plan. He knows exactly where you are and what you are experiencing. He is working in and through you at this very moment. The healing you so desire for your child may take longer than you ever expected. That's okay; don't lose heart. As you travel down this journey, cling to the presence of God, and trust Him with your very life, and with the life of your child. Look to the Word and to the Holy Spirit within you for assurance of the spiritual forces working in and around each and all of you. And sing praises to your Lord, for you are not alone.

The night after my daughter almost drowned at the pool, I sat down by her bed to tuck her in. 'Felicia, I am so thankful that you made it out of the pool okay today.'

'Me, too, Mommy.'

'But I have a question that just keeps nagging at me, how in the world did you get to the steps? I was watching you the whole time, and you were a good distance away from the steps when you fell in.'

Felicia looked at me with bright eyes and said matter-of-factly, 'Abigail must have helped me. I felt her hands grab under my arms and lift me up until my feet could touch the steps.'

Suddenly, everything was crystal clear to me. 'Oh, honey, that was not Abigail who lifted you to safety, for she didn't ever see you in the water. That was God who saved you today. It was all God!!' I'll never forget that. What a gift God gave Felicia that day, to not only literally, physically save her life, but to do it in such a way that she got to experience *feeling* His hands at work! She was exposed that day to the heavenly power of God as it manifested itself in our physical world. As I marveled at the reality of that, I realized that God had given me a gift as well: He showed me that He is present in the lives of our children, and that He loves our children so much that not a moment passes by that He does not notice. He taught me that I need to relax in my efforts to control the outcome of our children's lives, for their well-being, growth, protection, and future lives do not ultimately come from me, but from the Lord. God began that day to show me that I was consumed with fear. I believed that if I made enough mistakes in parenting, then I would mess up the lives of my children. God's work, however, is not dependent on our perfection. We are sinful and weak, but, thankfully, that does not deter God from fulfilling His purposes. Jeremiah 29:11 boldly tells us, *'For I know the plans I have for you, declares the LORD, plans to prosper you and not to harm you, plans to give you hope and a future.'* God is working out His perfect plans daily in the lives of our children. Yes, we play a part in those plans, but we do not determine the final outcome of their future. Because of that, we can breathe easier, and not fear. We are not alone. God is with us, leading the way.

Do not fear, for I am with you; do not be dismayed, for I am your God. I will strengthen you and help you; I will uphold you with my righteous right hand.
    ISAIAH 41:10

Personal Reflections:

1. Read Psalm 130:1-2, 5-7. Have you ever felt overwhelmed with life and parenting? Don't be afraid to lay all your anxieties before the Lord. He can take it! Talk to Him about your life, and seek His guidance.

2. Read Psalm 16:7-8. On the darkest of days, the Lord is right there with you. You are never alone. He is at your side, holding your hand, instructing you, and leading you down the paths He has set for you. Do not lose heart.

3. Read 2 Kings 6:8-17. If you are parenting a child who has experienced trauma and abandonment in any form, then chances are that you will come face-to-face with some extreme behavior. It is natural in those days to see only the dire circumstances surrounding you, and feel like you are in over your head. As you read these verses, I encourage you to ask God to lift your eyes to a broader, heavenly perspective of what is really going on in the life of your child. You are not alone. God is very present through it all.

4. Read John 10:10. Have you been listening to Satan's lies? He loves to discourage God's people and break families apart. Don't allow that to happen. Rather, cling to the promises that you have in Christ. Believe the words of Jesus, that He is working in you, and in your child, in order that you may both have abundant life. Think about that. What does Jesus mean? What kind of life and abundance is He talking about?

5. Read Jeremiah 29:11. These words apply to both you and your family. You may feel like your life is hard and unable to change. I know how that feels. I have been there. As you read and re-read Scripture, ask God to penetrate your heart so that you may believe His words are true. Believe He is telling the truth when He says that He does not desire to harm you. He wants to give you a future full of His good plans for you. Because of Christ's victory over death and His subsequent resurrection, we can have confidence that He is making all things new, restoring life, and giving hope.

5

Speaking Life

Extending Hope to Our Children

SOMETIMES all it takes is one small word to lift a heavy heart.

One Saturday afternoon, as I was thinking about what to make for dinner, I received an email from a neighbor. She knew that all of us were struggling as a family, and that each day we felt like we were walking on egg shells, not knowing what would trigger the next out-of-control episode from Carl. My nerves seemed to be constantly on edge. I had lost the joy I had so longed for in parenting, and had begun to wonder if Carl would ever find peace as a member of our family. It was right in the midst of this cloud of despair that the life-giving words came. My friend had no idea how much I needed hope at that moment; but God knew. I am sure that He was the one who nudged her to share with me what she had just witnessed.

It was warm outside that day, the kind of afternoon when children actually *want* to put aside their video games so they can run and play in the sunshine. A group of kids had gathered in front of my neighbor's house and decided to start an impromptu game of hide-and-seek. This was always a game they gravitated toward, for children of all ages could participate. On this particular day, the ages of the group ranged from five to fifteen. As soon as the game was suggested, everyone immediately began to shout, 'Not it!!' This had become their traditional way to get the game rolling.

In the midst of the group, however, there was one tiny little girl. She was about five years old, and had come over earlier that day for a play date with one of the neighborhood kids. Evidently, she had no idea that she was supposed to yell 'Not it!', so she quickly found herself 'It.' As everyone quickly dispersed to find hiding places, this girl just stood there with slumped shoulders and the look of dejection written all over her face. My friend was watching this play out from her porch. Not wanting this little girl to break down in a pool of tears right there in her front yard, she started to get up to go console the girl. Before she did, though, she noticed that Carl was also in her yard. He had chosen to not run off to hide as all the others had done. Instead, he quietly remained beside this sad little girl. My friend watched with interest, wondering what Carl was doing. As soon as everyone was out of sight, Carl leaned down toward the girl, reached out his hand, and said with a quick wink and a kind smile, 'Tag me. I'll be It.'

As my friend witnessed this small act of kindness that Carl offered to a young girl he did not know, her heart was warmed, for she saw the huge smile of appreciation that the girl gave to Carl as she tagged his hand. My friend delighted in witnessing the kindness that Carl was capable of when he did not feel stressed.

What a gift those words were to me that day. Not only did Carl's compassion breathe joy back into that young girl, but simply knowing that those events took place provided for me a calming stillness that washed over me like a balm. For the first time in a long time I felt peace, as I imagined Carl extending his hand and taking on the dreaded position of being 'It' so the little girl wouldn't have to. It's amazing how powerful tiny actions and words can be in the life of another.

But encourage one another daily, as long as it is called 'Today,' so that none of you may be hardened by sin's deceitfulness.

HEBREWS 3:13

What is it about words that affect us so much? I don't know about you, but I long to receive affirmation from others that I am doing something good and right. I cling to praises given to me, and roll them around in my head over and over, reliving every word spoken, taking in the warmth they bring to my heart. Proverbs 18:21 says that *'the tongue has the power of life and death.'* How often do we speak life-giving words to others? Some days when I am angry, hurt, or upset, it is easier to talk negatively against that person, sucking the life right out of them. When I am hurt, I don't want to impart life-giving words to that person; I want them to hurt right along with me. That is not what God has called us to do, though. He desires us to mirror Him instead, and breathe words of life.

From the beginning of the Bible, we are shown the power of words when God, Himself, literally speaks life into existence with the phrase, 'Let there be … .' Let there be light, let there be water, let there be plants and animals, and let there be man, made in the image of God. His powerful words do not end in Genesis, though; as the Bible unfolds, the words of God continue to speak life and grace into the lives of His people. For example:

+ *'The Lord then said to Noah, "Go into the ark, you and your whole family".'* (Gen. 7:1)—words of *protection*.

+ *'This is what the Lord, the God of Israel, says: "Let my people go".'* (Exod. 5:1)—words of *deliverance*.

+ *'I will take you as my own people, and I will be your God.'* (Exod. 6:7)—words of *belonging*.

+ *'I will surely bless you and make your descendants as numerous as the stars in the sky.'* (Gen. 22:17)—words of *promise*.

+ *'"Come follow me," Jesus said.'* (Matt. 4:19)—words of *invitation*.

+ *'Jesus told him, "Don't be afraid; just believe".'* (Mark 5:36)—words of *hope*.

+ *'Jesus said, "Father, forgive them, for they do not know what they are doing".'* (Luke 23:34)—words of *forgiveness*.

+ *'Jesus said, "Everything is possible for one who believes".'* (Mark 9:23)—words of *faith*.

+ *'You are looking for Jesus the Nazarene, who was crucified. He has risen! He is not here.'* (Mark 16:6)—words of *life*.

How sweet are your words to my taste, sweeter
than honey to my mouth!
PSALM 119:103 (ESV)

During the three years that Jesus' disciples spent with Him during His earthly ministry, they learned a great deal about how Jesus cared for the people around Him—especially those who had been marginalized. Jesus had a way of taking particular notice of these hurting people, extending genuine compassion to them, and helping them in ways that they needed most. The Bible records for us a magnificent instance in which Peter and John emulated these beautiful traits of Christ after the resurrection. They took notice of a man in need and, with compassionate hearts, were moved to help:

> *One day Peter and John were going up to the temple at the time of prayer—at three in the afternoon. Now a man who was lame from birth was being carried to the temple gate called Beautiful, where he was put every day to beg from those going into the temple courts. When he saw Peter and John about to enter, he asked them for money. Peter looked straight at him, as did John.*
>
> *Then Peter said, 'Look at us!'*
>
> *So the man gave them his attention, expecting to get something from them.*
>
> *Then Peter said, 'Silver or gold I do not have, but what I do have I give you.*
>
> *In the name of Jesus Christ of Nazareth, walk.'*

> *Taking him by the right hand, he helped him up, and instantly the man's feet and ankles became strong. He jumped to his feet and began to walk. Then he went with them into the temple courts, walking and jumping, and praising God.*
>
> ACTS 3:1-8

This story takes place as Peter and John are going about their everyday activities: *'One day Peter and John were going up to the temple at the time of prayer—at three in the afternoon.'* There were three different times throughout the day when Jews met at the temple for public prayer and worship, 9:00 a.m., 12:00 p.m., and 3:00 p.m. Before the two men entered the temple, they came to a crippled man, begging for money. *'Now a man who was lame from birth was being carried to the temple gate called Beautiful, where he was put every day to beg from those going into the temple courts. When he saw Peter and John about to enter, he asked them for money.'* For many of us, seeing someone panhandle from the side of the road is a common occurrence. The poor have always been with us, and, according to Jesus, always will be; at least on this side of heaven. Until we adopted Carl, I tended to pass these people by, intentionally looking the other way, ignoring their pleas. I can no longer do that, though; for, you see, Carl, from time to time, used to be one of those people.

In fact, this story pulls at my heart because not only does it introduce us to a man who needed to beg for money in order to live, but it also tells us that he was lame from birth. He had never enjoyed the ability and freedom to walk, but had to endure a life experienced from a mat on the ground. He was not able to know the fulfillment of doing a hard day's work, but rather was completely dependent on others to help him survive. In a somewhat similar way, Carl, too, was born crippled. No, his legs were not paralyzed, but his life had been harmed and stunted by the fact that he was born to parents who were dependent on drugs. Carl did not receive the attention he needed in order to grow and thrive as a child. From a very young age, Carl often found himself all alone on some street, digging through trash cans looking for food or items to sell, and holding out his hand, hoping for someone compassionate enough to give him some money to survive. I have never heard him tell me stories of feeling care-free and happy during this time in his life. His early childhood was not given the chance to thrive. Like the beggar on the mat, Carl was able to see people all around him live 'normal' lives, but had no way, on his own, to know how it felt to walk in those people's shoes.

Needing money to survive, the crippled beggar relied on the generosity of the people around him. So, as Peter and John came near, this man asked them for alms. Unlike many people who look the other way when they see needy people on the street, Peter and John looked at this man. I mean, they *really* looked at him, just like Jesus intently looked at the people He came across. Jesus did not see people as problems, but felt compassion for them. He was aware of the pain and struggles they faced in life. This, in turn, led Him to help in ways that He knew would be meaningful. Likewise, *'Peter looked straight at him [the beggar], as did John. Then Peter said, "Look at us!" So the man gave them his attention, expecting to get something from them.'* What he was about to receive, though, was not the usual gift of alms, but something far greater. He was about to receive a gift that would affect him for a lifetime, a gift that would be a constant reminder of

Jesus. *'Then Peter said, "Silver or gold I do not have, but what I do have I give you."'*

At this juncture, I find myself trying to imagine the face of the beggar. Was he curious about what the men had to offer? Was he disappointed for an instant? Was he tempted to look to another person walking by to ask them for money since it was obvious that these two men did not have any? I don't know, but I doubt that he expected to receive the gift that was being offered. *'"In the name of Jesus Christ of Nazareth, walk." Taking him by the right hand, [Peter] helped him up, and instantly the man's feet and ankles became strong.'* One simple phrase spoken in the name of Jesus changed this man forever.

In that instant, not only did he become physically strong, but he also became socially accepted. Among other things, he now had the ability to earn money to live, rather than beg. He could see people face-to-face, rather than always looking up from a mat. And, most importantly, he could join those going to the temple to pray, rather than sitting outside the gates, disconnected and alone. What a blessing this was when Peter and John took the time to enter into this man's life. They could have easily passed on by with no one thinking any less of them, and everything would have continued just as it always had. Thankfully, however, they stopped, saw his needs in life, and offered him the best they had, a new life through the power of Jesus.

These words of life proved to have immediate results in the life of the beggar. *'He jumped to his feet and began to walk. Then he went with them into the temple courts, walking and jumping, and praising God.'* At one moment he was bound to a mat, living in a position where he felt less valuable than those around him. The very next instant he was joyous, walking, jumping, and praising God. What a glorious transformation! He was literally given the ability to stand, which gave him the joy of feeling whole.

This scene might seem dramatic—like something that could only occur during the time of the Apostles. But is the effect any less significant when we take the time to speak words of life into the heart of a hurting child? A child who has gone through significant trauma, and who has experienced the deep pain of being abandoned by the very parents who should have loved him unconditionally, will often hold the belief that he is less than those around him. He may feel that he has very little value or worth. It is probable that he will think of himself as unlovable and unwanted, and his reactions to life may reflect this despair. Now, imagine someone coming over, putting her arm around this same child, telling him how special he is, and expressing her belief that he is going to do great things in life. What if this person tells him that no matter what that child says or does, she will always love him with a true, genuine love? How would that begin to bring healing into that child's life?

I Thessalonians 5:11 tells us to *'encourage one another and build each other up.'* Why are we told to do that? I believe it is because words hold great power. Our words can offer life and healing to people who are struggling, just as words of life were given to the beggar. When we help a child to understand that he was created in the image of God, and that his life has meaning to it, then he can begin to see himself in new ways he may have never considered before. Our words of love and encouragement should be a source of strength to help him stand as a child of God, and to see the great value and purpose his life has been given.

With five kids, some days I feel like all we are doing is going, going, going, and not enjoying being a family. Because of that, I decided not too long ago that it is important for us to set aside time to purposefully slow down and simply enjoy being together. There are two major ways we do this: first, Thursdays are now set aside as family game night, where we can team up in a round of Sorry, act silly with Charades, or fall all over each other laughing as we play Twister. It's refreshing to let loose and have fun, and it reminds us just how much we all enjoy being in a family together. Second, I have begun to schedule one-on-one time with everyone, so that each child gets my undivided attention one night per week at bedtime. This turns out to be about an hour of us sitting on the bed together, talking about life, God, or whatever comes to mind. In this small act, I have learned some incredible things about my children, and have been amazed more than once at how open and vulnerable they tend to be when given the opportunity.

One such night turned out to be an especially tender experience. For the first few years after joining our family, Carl struggled with his sense of worth. Because of that, I could tell that he was beginning to build his identity on some of the negative comments people had told him over the years, as well as on his own insecurities he felt about himself. Somehow I wanted to offer him a fork in the road to send him down a better path of knowing he was important and valuable to this world. As I was about to enter his room, I threw up a quick prayer. 'Lord, I don't know exactly what to say to Carl tonight, but he needs life-giving words. Would you please speak through me?' When I opened his door, I found him in bed, his light out, and his covers over his head, pretending to be asleep. It was obvious that he did not want to talk. That caused me to pause for a moment. I knew that he needed this time of interaction, though, so I turned the light on, and sat down beside him, praying that our time together would draw us closer as mother and son.

What happened in the next hour was absolutely beautiful. God led us from small talk, just getting our conversation started, to a stroll down memory lane. I love how God knew exactly what Carl needed at that moment. You see, even though Carl tends to have a tough exterior, God has shown me over and over that my son's heart is actually quite tender and loving, so I told Carl a few stories about his own life where I had noticed that he had been exceptionally kind to people. As I talked, he began to sit up and really listen, and he asked me over and over to tell him more stories where I had witnessed him doing something good for others. It was as if he were starved for someone to fill him up with truthful, encouraging words, and he drank in the words deeply.

At one point I took a break from the stories, and asked him if he could see that God had, indeed, created him to be a kind, sweet person who loved people. With bright eyes he said yes, he had always thought that way about himself. He just didn't think anyone around him could see that. Then the conversation brought in other wonderful aspects of who God made Carl to be.

He is a talented artist who loves to build and fix
    things.
He is a hard worker, and tries to do tasks to the best of
    his ability.
Little children are drawn to him because he interacts
    well with them.
And the list went on.

As the hour drew to an end, I praised God for the renewed life that he had breathed into both Carl and myself that evening through the power of words.

Kind words can be short and easy to speak, but their echoes are truly endless.

MOTHER TERESA

♦ *Words.* Simple little things that can build up or destroy a person at a moment's notice.

♦ *Words.* We tend to hang onto the words that have been spoken into our lives—good and bad. We need to be careful what we say to others.

♦ *Words.* God gives us his ultimate Word of Truth through Scripture, and Satan tries so hard to tear down those Truths with lies.

◊ Which will we believe?

◊ Which will we allow to penetrate our hearts?

◊ Which will we speak to our children?

♦ *Words.* Beautiful gifts of life. Don't keep them to yourself. Give them away generously.

Personal Reflections:

1. Read Hebrews 3:13. Has there ever been a time when you felt like your life was meaningless? What helped

you come out of that state of mind? Can you remember anyone who spoke encouraging, life-giving words to you? How can that experience help you to speak uplifting words to someone else who is struggling?

2. Read Psalm 119:103. God's Word is living and active and can give you the strength you need to carry on when you are in the midst of a difficult day. It offers healing words that speak truth into our souls, and can cover us like a sweet balm. How can we offer this gift to our children?

3. Read Proverbs 18:21a. What does this verse mean when it tells us that what we say can hold the power of life and death? I know from experience that raising a child who lived many years in dark places can prove to be challenging. As parents, are we spending more time reacting negatively to the actions of our child, or are we purposefully looking for places to speak blessing and encouragement into his life?

4. Read Acts 3:1-8. What can we learn from Peter and John in this scenario? Did they judge the beggar for sitting on his mat, trying to get something from others? Or did they understand his predicament in life, feel compassion for him, and offer him the words and power of Christ to help him? How can we emulate that with our broken children?

5. Read 1 Thessalonians 5:11. How can you encourage and build up your child in Christ today? Ask God to help you see beyond the difficulties of your child's behavior to the longing for encouragement in his heart. Regardless of how he reacts to your uplifting words initially, continue to daily feed him with words of life. He needs them, and over time they will make a difference.

6

The Gift of Story

Understanding the Importance of Our Own Life Chapters

STORY. Such a small, yet powerful, word. Stories have always been an important part of my life. I recall Granddaddy, who lived with us as I was growing up, telling me 'jigs,' which were funny little stories told in poem form that seemed to have no worthwhile meaning. Oh, but they did have meaning: they built a bridge of laughter and love between Granddaddy and me, as he came up with endless stories that never grew dull. I can still hear him now, 'Charlie Brown, went to town, riding a horse, leading a hound. Hound it barked, horse it jumped. Threw little Charlie Brown straddle of a stump.' Still makes me smile. Then there was Grandmother, who only knew two fairy tales. One about 'Little One Eye, Little Two Eye, and Little Three Eye,' and the other about 'Flopsy, Mopsy, and Cottontail.' I must have heard those stories told by her a million times; yet still, every time I spent the night, I longed to hear her tell them again.

There is something about a story that draws us in, piques our interest, and invites us to places we have never been. God gave us incredible minds that can imagine the tales we are told in such a way that brings the stories alive in full technicolor. It's no wonder He gave us the Bible, a book of stories more fanciful and intriguing than any other book around. It's a book about heroes and villains, kings and kingdoms, hostility and peace, bounty and loss, love and family, joy and sorrow, life and death. It's a book that invites us in and educates us about our beginnings, our brokenness, our purposes, and our futures. Unlike other stories, in a very real way, it breathes life into our aching souls, gives power to defeat spiritual foes, and explains to us who we are in this world. Amazingly, it also is a book that is still being written. God's story is not yet over. No, God is not still adding pages to Scripture, as that is complete; but He *is* still writing the story of creation, fall, redemption, and restoration on the pages of history. And we are very real characters, with very important purposes, in this incredible story.

For the longest time, I simply went through each day as if my life had no bearing on anything at all. I am convinced now, though, that every one of us has been given a life of great worth and meaning. I am humbled by that. 'Lord, mold me and use me in ways that help me fully realize my purpose for being. Use me for Your glory. Show me where to go, what to do, who to become, who to reach out to. Speak to me on the pages of my own story-board, so that I might follow Your will for my life, rather than my own self-centered desires. Show me, Lord, who You have created me to be all along. Illuminate to me parts of my life that have always shown patterns, gifts, longings, and dreams that have served to point me in the direction You would have me go. Make me more aware of who I am in You, and who You are in me, as we travel down this path of life together. I am not alone in this, am I? Thank You, Lord, for always being there, leading me, guiding me, loving me. Even when I was at my worst, You never booted me from your story.'

Ephesians 2:8-10 says *'For it is by grace you have been saved, through faith—and this is not from yourselves, it is the gift of God—not by works, so that no one can boast. For we are God's handiwork, created in Christ Jesus to do good works, which God prepared in advance for us to do.'* This entire verse is rich in meaning, but, as an artist, I am struck by one part in particular that speaks volumes to me: *'For we are God's handiwork, created in Christ Jesus …'*

We were hand-crafted by God. One translation says that we are God's masterpiece! When I create a painting or a sculpture, it is impossible for me to bring that piece of artwork to life without pouring myself into it. It becomes a very personal extension of who I am. So, when I think of God creating us, I never see it as something impersonal that just happened. No, who we were created to be is extremely personal and intentional. Therefore, taking the time to study Scripture, as well as looking back over our life-stories thus far, with the quest of trying to see more clearly who we are in Christ and how He has been working in our lives, has great value. Our stories are not meaningless, but useful for the playing out of God's ultimate plans.

Not all the pages of our stories are joyful, though. There are some chapters in our lives that we often wish we could just tear out and forget that they ever happened. Painful memories that still evoke deep emotions. Scars that we figured would disappear as we grew into an adult, but continue to remain. Feelings that come back on a moment's notice at some unexpected reminder of days past. We may ask ourselves why these things happened and whether there is any good that can come from them.

The ugliest scar that I carry around with me began to form in middle school. There was one year when my parents made the decision to take me out of the public school system in an effort to protect me from the world of drugs that had been introduced to my older sister. They wisely placed me in a local private Christian school, and were thankful for an opportunity to help me bypass the impending temptations that the particular public school in my home town held. I always enjoyed making new friends, so the prospect of changing schools did not bother me very much.

I remember the very first day Mom and Dad took me to see the school. We talked to the principal, walked around the campus, and then went into the office of the man who would be my teacher. He seemed to be kind and attentive, and assured all of us that he would take very good care of me. I recall listening to him talk, but the feelings that were stirring inside of me did not match what he was saying. He said he would take care of me, yet I felt leery of him. He said would teach me music at the school, but my churning stomach cautioned me to beware what else he wanted to teach me. In respect for my parents, however, and in respect to this teacher, I never voiced to anyone the concerns I had from that very first meeting. Rather, I put on a happy face and told myself I was just nervous about starting at a new school.

The next day I walked into the man's class, ready to be a part of this new life. Unfortunately, as time passed, this man did more than simply teach our class. He singled me out, and became unnaturally possessive of me. On the surface, he was kind, loving, and fun, but underneath it all he had a skewed perception of reality. During the next three years, I was increasingly placed in uncomfortable positions by this teacher as he became emotionally attached to me. Initially, I genuinely liked this man and was drawn to the personal attention he offered me. Over time, though, my fondness toward him changed into dread, and I looked for ways to avoid him; for his interest in me went well beyond what a healthy teacher/student relationship should look like. Many days, for instance, he beckoned me to stay alone in the classroom with him while the other children went outside to recess. During this time, he began sharing secrets with me, such as:

'Twila, I believe you are an angel who was sent by God to this school personally for me.'

'I thought you might like to know that my wife and I sleep in separate bedrooms.'

'I found this newspaper article about a teacher marrying one of his students. What are your thoughts about that?'

I never knew how I should respond to comments such as these, and was uncertain as to why he would tell them to me.

Back then, before the world of cell phones and texting, boys and girls would often pass notes to each other in an effort to flirt and to see if the other person was interested in them. In a similar manner, this teacher would write me little notes, fold them up, and give them to me in secret. Initially, I would answer him back with my own folded notes, simply in an effort to be nice. In my naiveté, I did not realize how abnormal our actions were, but later it hit me that we were playing the part of boy/girlfriend. Many other small things happened, each of them seemingly inconsequential when viewed alone, but when seen together, they added up to my being singled out and pursued in a way that was invisible to everyone around us. I knew something was not right with that behavior, but at such a young age, I was unable to pinpoint what, exactly, was wrong about it. I just knew that daily I lived on the uncertain edge of being afraid of what he would do next.

It seemed as if I would never get out from under this teacher's control, for each year as I progressed to new grade levels, he put in requests to teach the grade I was entering. After three years of his inappropriately pursuing me, something finally happened that allowed me to be free of him. I distinctly remember the very last day of school that particular year. By this time, my stomach would be in knots whenever he and I would be in the same room. Right before the end of that day, this teacher told everyone to line up, for he wanted to tell each of us goodbye. I cautiously watched as all the other kids lined up next to his desk, and he had each of the boys give him a hug, and each of the girls give him a kiss on the cheek. I thought I would throw up if I kissed him, so I backed up to the end of the line, trying to stay away for as long as I could. As each student hugged and/or kissed him and then left the classroom, I began to realize the mistake I had made. In taking a spot at the end of the line, I was setting myself up to be alone with him in the class. My heart began beating faster, and everything in me wanted to run away. But my sense of respect for people in authority over me was greater than my fear, so I stayed in the room. I recall vividly that when it was just the two of us left, he leaned his cheek toward me, waiting for my kiss. I remember looking at him and thinking his skin looked sweaty and slimy. The grin on his face was creepy. And the look in his eyes was seedy. 'Come on,' he said, 'give your favorite teacher a kiss goodbye.' So I leaned over to give him a quick peck on the cheek, but then he grabbed my face and forced me to kiss him smack-dab on the lips. I pulled away and ran as fast as I could out of there. I went to the restroom to wash my face and to try to stop crying. Thankfully, I had a friend who had suspected for a while that something was wrong between this teacher and me. She had compassion enough to ask me what had happened, then encouraged me to tell the principal, which I did. The teacher was immediately fired.

During those three school years, I hid what was going on from everyone because I feared that no one would believe me. As a result, I walked that painful path by myself, feeling isolated,

  alone,

    unimportant,

      and unable to change my situation.

I felt as meaningless to others as the dust in the dark under the teacher's desk. I was there for all those years, but no one saw the real me, nor what I was enduring. It felt like no one cared. Of course, if I had opened up to anyone about what was going on, they would have cared, but I did not have the courage to speak out. Rather, I felt this teacher held such a respected place in the school that I did not have a voice that anyone would hear and believe. After all, this teacher was a charming guy whom everyone liked. He was teaching at a Christian school, for goodness' sake! Certainly people would think I was making things up or misconstruing the facts. I was scared, and became highly emotional at odd places in my life. Things that shouldn't have upset me did, because I was breaking, I was fragile, and I didn't have any glue to hold me together.

I had thought all that was behind me, but it's not. One day, about a year after the adoption took place, Carl and I had a disagreement that resulted in me raising my voice to him, and him having an episode of exceptionally severe anger directed at me. For some reason, as that happened, I felt my cracks coming back. You know, I never did much during my childhood to bring about healing from the scars left by my teacher. I don't remember in my youth ever taking that burden to the Lord. I don't know why I didn't, though. It would have helped. Instead, I just painted pretty pictures over the top of my brokenness so no one would see the real me. Some of that paint chipped off on this particular day, however. I found myself getting more emotional than I thought possible, and I couldn't get a grasp on why that was happening. I was feeling isolated,

    alone,

       unimportant,

          and unable to change my situation.

In other words, I felt the same way I had with that teacher. You see, back then, no one ever saw what happened behind closed doors, so they could not help me when I needed help the most. Likewise, Carl, in his own trauma, did not allow any other adult to see his out-of-control self, except for me. For the longest time, even Jeff had not witnessed the full force of it firsthand. So, I found myself feeling alone, without anyone present to help me when I needed it the most. That awful feeling I had had as a little girl had the gall to come back into my life! That is, until Jeff lovingly spoke truth to me. You see, many days when Carl and I butted heads, I would call Jeff for support. His gentle voice and calm demeanor helped both of us tremendously. Occasionally, when Carl's anger would reach frightening levels, Jeff would even come home from work early to help mitigate and diffuse the situation.

On this particular day, after Carl had calmed down, Jeff then turned to me to privately address my own brokenness. He said, 'Twila, you are trying to help a Post-Traumatic-Stress child, but I think that you, too, are a Post-Traumatic-Stress victim who needs help.' How did he know? Was my paint that transparent to him? I so wanted everyone to see a façade of togetherness in my life. Was it possible that he could he see my cracks and sense that I was on the verge of completely falling apart? I praise God for Jeff, because his willingness to say that had already encouraged me more than I could express. He helped me pick up the broken pieces of my life and beckoned me to lay them at the foot of the cross. He prayed with me and for me over my struggles. He saw me for who I was, even with all my hurts and weaknesses, and loved me anyway. When that happened, I saw God reflected in Jeff.

That afternoon I read something on Facebook that said, 'Don't look for someone who will solve all your problems. Look for someone who won't let you face them alone.' Thank you, Jeff, for faithfully being there by my side.

Once I had a moment to reflect, I could begin to see what God was up to with all this fear and mental anguish. He was opening up my eyes to see where Carl is on days when he is out of control. Carl did not have only three years of abuse like I did, but twelve. His painful experiences did not begin when he was a pre-teen, but when he was an infant. So, his cracks are deeper and longer than mine ever were, and parts of him have already broken. It's no wonder that certain words and situations trigger intense reactions within him. As I further processed how the perverted actions of my teacher negatively affected my life, I began to notice a striking similarity between Carl and myself. When his dark memories surfaced, they sparked intense fear-reactions inside of him, driving him away from the hope that he could fit into the family unit. When that happened, he retreated, and felt isolated,

   alone,

    unimportant,

     and unable to change his situation.

As God illuminated to me the hopelessness that Carl felt, I found I could relate to him, for during my childhood, I had often experienced that same emotion. All of a sudden, I could see that Carl's actions were not intentionally rebellious ones, but natural responses of a person who had been deeply hurt. For the first time in my life, I was thankful for the gift of a difficult past, for God used it to give me a great empathy, understanding, and compassion for my son that went deeper than the surface. I found myself desiring to tell Carl that the horrific things that had been done to him by various people in his life were not his fault. I wanted him to understand that even though he had been hurt in his past, God had not only delivered him from those abusers, but had placed him in a safe, loving environment. And, I longed for him to know how important it was in life to try to look to the future with hope and expectation rather than to stay mired in the past experiences of fear and dread, like I had done for too many years.

'Thank You, Lord, for using this painful experience from my past to give me the perspective to see Carl in a new light. You have redeemed that broken part of my life, haven't You, Lord? You have transformed it from a rocky path into a glorious bridge of understanding between Carl and myself. Only You could do something like that. Now show me, Lord, how to walk across this bridge, how to be Carl's glue, how to be there for him in ways that will help hold him together, while You are in the midst of doing the real miracle of restoring him and making him new.'

'He will wipe away every tear from their eyes, and death shall be no more, neither shall there be mourning nor crying nor pain anymore, for the former things have passed away.' And he who was seated on the throne said, 'Behold, I am making all things new.'

REVELATION 21:4-5 (ESV)

I have experienced pages in friends' lives that were brimming with anticipation and celebration. We rejoiced together on those sparkling days, giving God all the praise. I have also seen pages in lives that were soggy with continual tears, and still others that were worn so thin with the heavy pressures of life that we wondered how those pages were holding together. When we experience challenging days like that, it is often difficult to lift up praise and worship to our Father in heaven. As strongly as we grasp the joyful days, we find that eventually they fall from our clutches, throwing us into challenging ones. On those days, I keep my Bible open to the Psalms, where David's honest, heartfelt words resonate with my hurting soul. *'Save me, O God! For the waters have come up to my neck. I sink in deep mire, where there is no foothold; I have come into deep waters, and the flood sweeps over me. I am weary with my crying out; my throat is parched. My eyes grow dim with waiting for my God'* (Ps. 69:1-3 ESV).

Have you ever felt like that? Completely overwhelmed with the pressures of life. How do you navigate those waters? What do you do when unthinkable events come crashing into your life? I have friends who were told, one week before flying to another country to adopt their children, that the birth mother had returned and wanted the children back. I recall watching my friend struggle as she sought to find the Lord's guidance in how she ought to move forward from that place of despair. Other families have also experienced deep heartache when their plans to adopt from Russia were halted because the door connecting them was slammed shut. How do you move on with news like that? What about families who adopted, only to find the mental anguish of the child was so great that he posed a very real threat to the safety of everyone in the home? Or what of the children who have Reactive Attachment Disorder (RAD), which causes them to be incapable of bonding? Or what about those few adoptions that ultimately are dissolved? How does a family process a tragedy like that? How do you keep going when you are lying on the floor of despair, not knowing how to get back on your feet? The bottom line is, it is not easy.

Unfortunately, on this side of heaven, we live in a world permeated by the effects of sin. The Bible tells us that with sin comes all kinds of difficulties such as sickness, death, rebellion, separation, pain, and darkness. That is not the end of the story, though. As a child of God, that is *never* the end of the story. God, you see, is writing and directing the entire sweep of history, which encompasses the whole picture of creation, fall, redemption, and restoration. Amazingly, this includes our own personal life stories. I know that there are seasons in our lives when we can squint as hard as we can but are still not able to make out any semblance of light ahead of us. Those days can feel awfully cold and suffocating. Thankfully, though, God's goodness and presence in our lives are not reliant on our emotions, but on His character. We must cling tightly to Him, for He is our lifeline and the One who will ultimately work all this out for our good and His glory.

... the Spirit helps us in our weakness. For we do not know what to pray for as we ought, but the Spirit himself intercedes for us with groanings too deep for words. And he who searches hearts knows what is the mind of the Spirit, because the Spirit intercedes for the saints according to the will of God. And we know that for those who love God all things work together for good, for those who are called according to his purpose.

ROMANS 8:26-28 (ESV)

An inspiring account of God's hand at work in the life of a hurting family is recorded in Mark 9:14-29. I am thankful that the Bible gives us true stories such as this one from which we can draw strength. Parents throughout time have struggled in ways similar to ourselves, because raising children has always induced a certain amount of stress. Bringing up children who are affected by traumatic experiences in their lives adds extra levels of anxiety and concern. This story is one many of us can relate to, for it speaks of a family with a son who is going through life with issues heavier than most children bear. For years, the child in this story had an unclean spirit controlling him, stealing his speech, throwing him into convulsions, and threatening to take his life. This might not mirror exactly what our own children are experiencing, but in some ways it may. For example, have you ever felt like there was a spiritual battle warring in the heart of your child? Do triggers from your child's past trauma ever propel him to intense levels of acting out? Does he ever retreat to places where he seems unable to communicate with anyone? Does he ever try to hurt himself in an effort just to feel something? If you can answer 'yes' to any of these questions, or others like them, then I encourage you to ask God to speak to your heart as you walk down the path of this story. In these verses, you will come to know a father and son duo who are struggling to survive the difficulties of life. The father has been able to love and protect his child for years, but he has not been able to heal the heart of his son's particular problem. As he comes face-to-face with Jesus, however, he learns that the Lord is the only One capable of helping his son by changing him from the inside, out.

Every time I read this story, I find myself feeling the heaviness that is pulling down this father, the love he has for his struggling son, and the impact their experiences have had on others, like myself, throughout time. All evidence points to the fact that this father was living a life of desperation, for the challenges his son faced daily seemed insurmountable. His years of parenting difficulties, however, were not without purpose in the grand scheme of life, for in the end, they brought glory to the Lord Jesus Christ and gave hope to other parents dealing with intense struggles with their children.

It is significant that this encounter occurred as soon as Jesus had come down from the mountain of transfiguration where God audibly proclaimed, *'This is my beloved son; listen to him'* (Mark 9:7). Since there are no coincidences in the Bible, I am led to believe that the words Jesus says to the father and his son in this situation are words we would be wise to follow in our own lives. Sometimes it is easy to read through accounts in the Bible and see them only as stories, disconnected from our own realities. The truth of the matter, though, is that while they are, indeed, portions of people's lives who lived thousands of years ago, those experiences were divinely recorded in order to reach across time and influence our lives today.

As Jesus literally came off an incredible mountaintop experience, He walked directly into a heated situation involving His disciples, teachers of the law, a father, and his son. What a stark descent from the glorious meeting with Moses and Elijah to the harsh realities of this sin-indwelt world. As Jesus entered this scene, He zeroed in on the quarreling that was taking place, asking the most basic of questions, *'What are you arguing with them about?'* (v. 16).

Why do any of us argue? I know that I tend to argue most when things are not going my way, or when I feel threatened in some way. When I think I am in the right or am not being respected, or when I am stressed and tired, I tend to be more argumentative. The book of James explains arguments quite pointedly, *'What causes quarrels and what causes fights among you? Is it not this, that your passions are at war within you? You desire and do not have, so you murder. You covet and cannot obtain, so you fight and quarrel'* (James 4:1-2a ESV). So, why were they arguing? The answer came not from Christ's disciples, but from the man most desperate for help and answers, the father of a suffering son. *'Teacher, I brought you my son, who is possessed by a spirit that has robbed him of speech. Whenever it seizes him, it throws him to the ground. He foams at the mouth, gnashes his teeth and becomes rigid. I asked your disciples to drive out the spirit, but they could not'* (vv. 17-18).

So, here is a father who had spent years of his life trying to protect and care for a child who was at the mercy of an unclean spirit. Day and night, this faithful father had given his constant attention to the son whom he loved, to the son who had challenges different from others, to the son who was probably pushed aside by most of society because of the odd ways the demon controlled him. How tired this man must have been! I can just imagine the ray of hope he felt, though, when he heard that Jesus was in town. Could it be that he had finally found an answer to his son's struggles? As he was drawn by the Spirit to the presence of the Lord, we can picture him immediately responding in faith by taking his son's hand and journeying together to Jesus. What a beautiful picture that paints for us in how we are called to parent, walking through life together, hand in hand, leading our children to Christ.

As this father sought out Jesus, he found the disciples instead. This was not a bad thing, however, for the disciples had been known to heal people in the name of Jesus. They were the next best thing, impressive authorities in drawing out unclean spirits, with proven track records. Unfortunately, though, as hard as they tried, the disciples were incapable of drawing the spirit out of this particular boy. In turn, this prompted the teachers of the law to ridicule the apparent failure of the disciples, causing an argument to ensue. As they argued, I wonder what happened to the heart of the father. Just moments before, his faith and hope for healing had soared, and now, with the quick turn of events of the disciples' inability to heal the son, I wonder if the father's hope wavered. Did he believe he had reached the end of his rope, and that all hope for healing was lost? Sometimes we, too, place our hope in methods of parenting that worked for another family, but are not effective with our own. Or, we assume certain people are the highest authorities regarding the conditions of our children, only to find that these well-meaning people cannot provide any real help. It can be disheartening, can't it? Don't lose hope, though! Allow the rest of this story to touch your aching heart, and to revive an expectant spirit within you, because Jesus is making His way onto the scene; and with Jesus present, all things are possible.

After hearing the father's account of what had happened, Jesus rebuked the unbelief stirring in the hearts of people, then tenderly sought out the son: *'Bring the boy to me'* (v. 19). As I apply this story to modern times, I realize that Jesus is saying that same thing to us. He wants us to fight against the unbelief that often pools inside of us, and willingly guide our children to Him, to teach them about Him, to bring them to the cross, to surrender them to His care. Yet I have challenges doing this, for as soon as I start nudging my children to trust in Jesus, I find myself also hanging on desperately to their coat tails, afraid that if I let them go entirely, then my loss of control will somehow be to their detriment. Do I really trust the love Jesus has for my children? Do I truly believe that He is both willing and able to help my children in ways that I cannot? Or am I more like this father who responds to Jesus by saying, *'... if you can do anything, take pity on us and help us'* (v. 22)? *If* you can do anything? That tiny word 'if' holds so much uncertainty in it. Since the father's initial hope for healing had been squelched by the disciples' inability to make a change in his son, perhaps he now questioned if anyone, including Jesus, could help his particular situation. He may have wondered if his son's challenges were unique, more difficult to remedy than others. Jesus heard the combination of plea and doubt in the words of this father, and immediately, lovingly, helped correct his skewed perspective.

"'If you can?" said Jesus. "Everything is possible for one who believes'" (v. 23). Can you imagine how the father's countenance must have lifted at that point? Hope came pouring back into his weary soul, and he instantly exclaimed, *'I do believe'* (v. 24). He so wanted to accept the possibility that Jesus could, indeed, heal his precious son, that he reacted by boldly proclaiming his belief. But in the very next instant, another side of him sent up a red flag, and he added an honest, vulnerable statement of *'help me overcome my unbelief'* (v. 24). As much as I would like to proclaim myself a person of faith who never wavers or doubts the power of Christ in my life, the truth of the matter is that many, many days I simply hang on to a thread of faith to make it through. A drop of faith, though, can move mountains. No matter how insignificant the

father's faith seemed, Jesus knew that great power resided in that inkling of belief. This was not the power of human ability, but the power that comes solely from the Lord above.

Jesus then looked at the demon-possessed boy and rebuked the dark spirit within him. *"'You deaf and mute spirit … I command you, come out of him and never enter him again." The spirit shrieked, convulsed him violently and came out'* (v. 25). After this great crescendo, I imagine everything was as quiet as snow, with all eyes glued on the boy. The father's heart was probably pounding, and his hope of healing had surely hit an all-time high. Jesus was, indeed, the Great Physician, the only One capable of touching his son's life in such a transformative way. Can't you hear his heart screaming with great conviction now: 'I believe!'?

It appeared as if something was wrong, though. The boy just laid there. In fact, *'the boy looked so much like a corpse that many said, "He's dead." But Jesus took him by the hand and lifted him to his feet, and he stood up'* (v. 27). In an instant, Jesus vanquished the evil spirit from the boy, giving him strength, clarity of mind, dignity, and the chance to begin life as a healed, restored child. What a memorable day that was! I can only imagine the joy that must have surged through the father and son. Prayers had been answered as they came face-to-face with Jesus. Who knew when they woke up that morning that the course of their lives would change so dramatically in just a few short hours? No doubt, they were full of gratitude toward Jesus and eager to share the good news with family and friends.

After all the excitement began to die down, and the father took his son home, the disciples gathered around Jesus and asked Him, *'Why couldn't we drive [the spirit] out?'* (v. 28). Jesus' answer was simply, *'This kind can come out only by prayer'* (v. 29). Of all the strong emotions, drama, twists, turns, and resolution that this story offers, my favorite portion is this line by Jesus, telling His disciples how, exactly, that particular boy was healed. You see, Jesus not only created the boy, but He was and is mighty in power, omniscient, King of kings, and Lord of lords. He did not have to try various methods to see which one would cause the unclean spirit to come out. He knew all along exactly what it would take. He did not have to question His abilities, for He holds all the answers to every situation in His hands.

Do you know what that means for you? Jesus knows you and your child intimately, and He knows the long-term answer to what is troubling you. He is actively working out His plans in you, and through your lives. Even if you cannot yet see the fruit of His work, you can rest assured that He is present. Do not become discouraged by what your eyes see, nor by the length of time it is taking for healing to occur. In the end, the healing may not look like what you had hoped for, but it will be the outcome determined by our heavenly Father, who is good and wise. Trust Him. His ways, you see, are not our ways (Isa. 55:8), and He does not view events linearly like we do. Rather, He works all things together, throughout history, in ways that we cannot fully understand. He is the God who is able to turn past abuses into bridges of love; He allows our life experiences to touch the lives of others whom we may not even know; He redeems and uses our life stories; and He integrates them into the beautiful masterpiece of history. Rest in that.

All of this is one way of saying that life is so worth living! Our individual life stories are important. God has walked with us down beautiful paths and deep gullies so that we might see Him more clearly in all aspects of life. In every circumstance He is present, working out His intricate tapestry, which stretches throughout time. I look to the future with absolute certainty that God is personally, actively writing the pages of my life's story, as well as Carl's, with a grand purpose. Our stories now share many of the same pages, and are filled with pain and healing, confusion and clarity, sorrow and joy, mistakes and forgiveness. We are family. I do not yet know the words, characters, or plots of the next chapter, but I do know some of the themes of the story. We are to use all the experiences in our lives, good and bad, to grow closer to our Lord, Jesus Christ, and we are to compassionately reach out to each other as we struggle in the brokenness of this world. We are to trust God and seek His counsel throughout life. We are to listen to each other, love well, and pray fervently, all with the grand intention of tilting chins up a bit to see God's presence in our lives. The enemy so loves to discourage God's people. I believe part of what God has created us for is to show people hope in the One who loves them, giving them a new perspective in life. This helps them see that they, too, are important characters in God's eternal story.

Personal Reflections:

1. Read Ephesians 2:10. Have you thought about the fact that you were hand-crafted by God? He intentionally made you just the way you are in order that you may be able to best fulfill your callings in life. What is unique about you? What gifts, talents, and passions has He placed inside of

you? In what ways is God using you to touch the lives of others?

2. Read Psalm 69:1-3. We all have days in our lives where we feel completely overwhelmed with the pressures of life. David models for us, through the Psalms, just how raw we ought to be with God. It is okay to lay our concerns and emotions out there for God to see. He is not surprised by them, nor does He condemn us for our weaknesses. Rather, this type of vulnerability draws us into a closer relationship with Him, for He listens with great care and comforts us when we need it. Is there anything weighing on your shoulders right now that you need to talk to God about? Pull up a chair and begin a conversation with Him. He is patiently waiting for you.

3. Read Romans 8:26-28. Do you know with great certainty that God is working all things out for the good of those who belong to Him? Many days, you may struggle to believe that. When it seems as if your life is crashing in on you, remember that God is actively working, and that at some point in time, you will be able to see the fruit of His work. Just be patient, for God is never in a hurry to fulfill His plans, but rather works in His perfect timing.

4. Read Mark 9:24. Do you ever wonder if your faith is so weak that God cannot use you? This verse is a strong reminder that even the tiniest amount of faith can be used mightily by God. Can you recall a time in your life when He touched your life in some way, even though your faith was weak? Praise Him for that, and allow it to strengthen you the next time you struggle

144

7

Restoring Hope
Looking Forward with Great Joy and Expectation

WHETHER we notice them or not, God fills our lives with blessings, gifts we don't deserve, and beautiful additions that add depth and dimension. I have missed many of these blessings over the years as I struggled with fear, depression, and anxiety. One particular gift, however, stood out so strongly in my childhood years, that I grabbed hold of it then with my tiny little heart. To this day, I am still enjoying the beauty and meaning of it. That blessing was a special relationship with my Granddaddy, which formed after he and Grandmother moved in with us when I was young. I remember coming home from school every day, and immediately running downstairs to the waiting lap of Granddaddy. There was so much warmth and security in his presence that I found myself desiring— needing—to daily soak in his love. I told him all about the silly, inconsequential details of my day, and he taught me a myriad of things such as how to garden, love family, make slingshots from tree branches, carve monkeys from peach seeds, and live for Christ. He told me jokes to make me laugh and held my hand to make me smile. When I think about him so many years ago, my heart still warms, and my memories of him easily return. What a blessing he was to me.

As much as I loved Granddaddy, Grandmother loved him even more. They had a sweet relationship that modeled for me the beauty of marriage-for-life. They enjoyed each other whether they were planting vegetables together, watching TV, or taking care of each other during sickness. In his last few years, Granddaddy's body became frail and worn out, and Grandmother willingly devoted herself to giving him the constant, tender care he needed. As the end of Granddaddy's days grew near, he laid quietly in his bed, completely deaf by now to most of the world around him, weak, and dependent on Grandmother for everything. Grandmother's heart ached at the thought of life without her husband, so she hung tightly onto every moment she had left with him.

About a week before Granddaddy met Jesus face-to-face, God opened up the windows of heaven in his cozy little bedroom. On that memorable day, Grandmother was in another room when she heard Granddaddy call out to her, 'Lena! What is that music?' Confused about what he was saying, Grandmother walked to the bedroom and said,

'Joe, what are you talking about?'

'That music … can't you hear it?'

'There is no music playing, Joe. The TV is off, and the radio is off. It's perfectly quiet. What are you talking about?'

'It's beautiful, Lena. Can't you hear it? It's the most beautiful music I have ever heard! It's bright, clear, and strong. You can't hear it?'

No, she couldn't, but she could look at Granddaddy's radiant face and tell that he was privy to something wonderful and miraculous. She was confident that God had opened Granddaddy's deaf ears to give him a foretaste of what it would be like to hear the music of heaven with healed ears. Many times throughout that day, Granddaddy heard the music; and every time he did, Grandmother was given the gift of hope and assurance that heaven was a reality, and that God was already gently ushering Granddaddy into his new home.

Hope is an incredible, powerful thing in our lives. It gives us a reason to keep going when life is difficult. It is a reminder that this life, clouded by sin and pain, is not our final experience. It gives us confidence that we can trust our Lord, for He is the One who loves to rescue, restore, and redeem our broken lives.

Hope: A strong and confident expectation—(Bible.org)

For in hope we were saved. Now hope that is seen is not hope, because who hopes for what he sees? But if we hope for what we do not see, we eagerly wait for it with endurance.
ROMANS 8:24-25 (NET)

Sometimes the gift of hope is clearly seen and understood, as was the case with my grandparents. Other times, however, we may be struggling so much that we feel as if the possibility of a better future has bypassed us altogether. Or, maybe, our children are so captured by the heartaches of their past that it seems as if they will never break free from those chains. As I look back over the threads of biblical history, it is evident that we are not the only ones who have experienced this sense of hopelessness. Adam and Eve, for example, must have felt despondent when God sent them from the Garden of Eden. Joseph despaired when his brothers sold him into slavery. Certainly, the disciples were mournful when Jesus was crucified.

God, however, knew that all was not lost in the lives of each of these people. He purposefully banished Adam and Eve from the garden to protect them from eating from the Tree of Life. Doing so would have caused them to eternally live in sin. Before they left, He gave them the promise of a Savior to come. This Savior, Jesus, would crush the head of the serpent and offer a way back to an even better garden. God allowed Joseph to be taken away to a foreign land as a slave and to be imprisoned for years. He did not do this to be cruel, but to place Joseph in a unique, surprising position from which he would be given the opportunity to interpret the Pharaoh's dreams. This, in turn, would elevate Joseph to a position of great power, through which he could later help God's people survive. And, finally, as Jesus was taken away to be nailed to a Roman cross, His disciples dispersed in fear. After His death was complete, I am certain that His disciples felt deeply morose and defeated. The three days when Jesus lay silent in a tomb were assuredly the darkest, most disheartening days that the disciples had ever experienced. God knew what was on the horizon, though. The disciples were blind with grief, but God was very aware of the plan He was working out, a plan of new life, of redemption, of renewed hope. It just took time. The disciples' only option was to walk through the dark days in order to arrive at the glorious days that God knew were coming. We, too, must sometimes walk through our own dark days, or months, or years, in order to reach the place where God wants to take us.

In similar fashion, when the Israelites were overtaken and exiled to Babylon, they were forced to walk through many years of difficult life experiences. In the midst of this dark time in their history, God spoke words of promise and encouragement into their aching hearts. Interestingly, these words have the ability to touch our lives today just as powerfully as they did for the Israelites back then. One small sampling from this era that has encouraged me is from Isaiah 43:18-19:

> *Remember not the former things,*
> *nor consider the things of old.*
> *Behold, I am doing a new thing;*
> *now it springs forth, do you not perceive it?*
> *I will make a way in the wilderness*
> *and rivers in the desert* (ESV).

In the verses leading up to this passage, Isaiah reminded the Israelites of how God's mighty acts of deliverance had led their people out of slavery in Egypt years before. This rescue, however, was not an easy path for the Israelites to tread, for they experienced times of uncertainty and fear. As the Israelites exited Egypt, for example, they quickly found themselves in a situation that appeared to have no way out: the Egyptian army was pursuing them from behind, and the enormous Red Sea stood before them, blocking their way of escape. God, however, provided a way out, miraculously parting the Red Sea and allowing the Israelites to cross through to the other side on dry ground. He then engulfed the Egyptian army in the waters when they tried to follow suit. What an amazing heritage to remember! The Lord loved them, took them as His own, and saved them from certain doom. Just when things looked the worst, God made a way of escape and delivered His people from the very things they feared.

Generations later, when Israel found herself in exile, captured by another nation, God continued to show His love and care for her. I can see the Israelites now, raptly listening to Isaiah deliver God's message. My guess is that, as Isaiah recapped the exodus out of Egypt, the Israelites expected him to end his story with a proclamation that God was going to deliver them now from the clutches of Babylon in similar fashion. How exciting it would be to experience, first hand, the miracles of God!

Isaiah, however, catches them off guard, telling them to *forget* the things of the past. *'Remember not the former things, nor consider the things of old.'* What do you mean, Isaiah? We don't want to let go of those stories, for we are hoping with everything in us that those very things will happen to us, too! Are you saying that there is no hope for us, that God has turned His back on us and walked away? No, that was not at all the message that was to be delivered to the Israelites that day. Rather, they were given a message of great hope for *new* things to come. *'Behold, I am doing a new thing; now it springs forth, do you not perceive it?'* Sometimes we cling so tightly to what we want and expect out of life, and out of the lives of our children, that we are blind to new ways in which the Lord is working. Here, God is claiming that He is about to do something so grand and extraordinary that it will eclipse the grandeur of the exodus out of Egypt. What He did back then will be nothing in comparison to what He is starting now.

'I will make a way in the wilderness and rivers in the desert.' The wording of this statement is fascinating, for it is juxtaposed against Isaiah's description of the exodus out of Egypt. During that deliverance, God parted the waters and led them through the seabed on dry land. Now, however (as someone once pointed out to me), He is saying something quite the opposite: the deliverance that is about to take place will not be through a body of water, but through the desert. And rather than giving the gift of dry ground in the middle of the sea to walk on, He will bring forth rivers in the desert where there were none before. Yes, God is setting the stage not only to take His people back home, but also to offer them redemption through faith in Christ. He is giving them a vision of what is to come. He is giving them *hope*!

The trek back home, though, will involve physically and spiritually going through the heat and desolation of the desert. It will not be easy. In fact, at this point in history, the Israelites had been in Babylon for so long that many of the people who were being expected to journey to Israel had been born there, in exile. It was the only life they had ever known, so, even though the path of a better future was laid before them, it would be a long, unfamiliar road to the home where they belonged.

Similarly, earlier in their lives, our adopted children, too, were forced into their own lands of exile. For one reason or another, all of which are tragic, these children had to leave their birth parents and enter into a different world, carrying the weight of being orphans. For many, this life was full of fear and uncertainty, yet one which would eventually become their 'new normal.'

As God called our children out of their orphan status into their new homes, most found it was more difficult than expected to leave the life they were most familiar with behind. That old life had become a part of who they were, so the experiences and feelings of being an orphan were packed right alongside their belongings and moved with them to their new homes. This reality, in turn, brought our children to us with walls of fear encasing them, causing trust and togetherness as a family unit to initially be difficult to achieve. God's words in Isaiah, however, continually speak to these unstable dynamics, offering whispers of hope: *'I will make a way in the wilderness and rivers in the desert.'* Yes, we have our own wildernesses to venture through as we work to create a strong family, but we are never traveling through them alone. As we follow God's lead, we can hang on to the fact that He will be with us every moment. Not only that, but somewhere along the way, God will bring relief from the elements in the wilderness. He will quench our thirst with the cool water we long for, giving us all that we need to complete the journey. In doing so, He will remind us that He is our provider and sustainer. He is all we need.

Let's pause here for just a moment to consider what is being said. On one level, it is easy enough to agree with the fact that God is with us, helping us, and providing all that we need to parent our children well. On a practical level, though, what does that look like? Are we supposed to sit back and expect that God will magically work everything out without our doing anything? Should we strive to parent through difficult situations apart from the world around us, simply hanging on to our devotion books? No, I do not believe that was ever God's intention for us. Certainly, we need to read our Bibles and develop our relationship with God, but there is even more available to us. We need to connect with the community God has placed around us. For God's means of provision quite often come through other people.

Jeff and I learned that the hard way. Initially, we thought we could handle everything on our own. Somehow, it felt like if we reached out to others for advice, or went the more formal route of seeking professional family counseling, we would be admitting that we were failures. The truth of the matter, though, is that we ended up putting on a pretty front out in public for the world to see, while struggling more than we ever thought possible in the solitude of our home. Help was all around us, but we chose to ignore it. We had friends who were walking down similar paths of adoption, yet we said we didn't have the time to meet and talk with them. Our church offered free counseling for Jeff and me, as well as for our children, yet we kept putting that off, saying things really weren't all that bad. Books gave some practical help, but they could not give us a hug and a personal prayer like a friend could do. It wasn't until we found ourselves in a desperate situation that we finally reached out for help. Once that happened, we were humbled and amazed by the comfort friends willingly gave, and by the wise counsel our pastor provided. It was at that point that Jeff and I saw the great value in being vulnerable with others, and letting them know how we were struggling. I wish we would have done that years earlier.

Honestly, a large part of the reason why it took us so long to seek help was because of me. I thought, for some reason, that reaching out to others wasn't very Christ-like. My natural inclination has always been to counsel *other* people with their challenges and heartaches in life, not to *be* the one receiving help. I had no problem understanding that *God's* grace was sufficient for me, and that His power was made perfect in my weakness (2 Cor. 12:9), but I did not want to be the one to proclaim my weaknesses to other *people*. I struggled with that, though, because a part of me really wanted to open up to someone else who would listen, but I could not find a Bible verse that confirmed that that was a godly thing to do. In my mind, all the verses about help and encouragement seemed to either cry out to *God* for help, or they were written from the stance of being the one to *give* others help.

'Hear my cry, O God, listen to my prayer …'
(Ps. 61:1).

'Comfort one another …' (1 Thess. 4:18 asv).

'Encourage one another and build each other up'
(1 Thess. 5:11).

'Bear one another's burdens, and so fulfill the law of Christ' (Gal. 6:2 esv).

'And we urge you, brothers, admonish the idle, encourage the fainthearted, help the weak, be patient with them all' (1 Thess. 5:14 esv).

I interpreted these verses to say that, as followers of Christ, we were to be the ones giving the comfort, encouragement, and help, not the ones needing it. Of course, I was wrong in my interpretation. I was ignoring the words 'one another, each other,' and 'brothers.' The help was to go both ways. We are to give *and* receive it.

It wasn't until God brought to my mind a passage about *Jesus* needing help, however, that I was willing to admit that I had been wrong. After Jesus had been betrayed by Judas, He entered into a physically and emotionally grueling time in His life. He was arrested, testified against, condemned, spat on, blindfolded, beaten, denied, flogged, mocked, and handed over to be crucified. The Romans required that the prisoners condemned to die carry the horizontal bar of their own instrument of death to the place of execution. By this time, though, Jesus had endured so much physically that He was unable to carry His beam the entire distance. He needed help. Did you hear that? *Jesus* needed help! So, when a man who was in close proximity to Jesus was told to carry the cross for Him, Jesus let him help (Mark 15:21). He did not fight him off, saying He could do it Himself. He did not boast that He was the all-powerful God of the universe, so He could carry the cross Himself. Nor did He indicate any shame in being helped. I truly believe that God knew that Jesus was at His breaking point, so He lovingly sent a man who 'just happened to be passing by' to give a bit of relief to Jesus. And Jesus accepted the help. He probably breathed a sigh of relief, even, when that physical burden was momentarily lifted off His shoulders. It is important to note that this aid did not lessen Jesus' calling; rather, it helped Him to fulfill it. As I read those words, I realized that not only is it *okay* to seek out help when we need it, but it is wise and good and a blessing from God.

So, I want to encourage you who feel like you are drowning to not be afraid to shoot up a flare, indicating to others your great need for help. There is no shame in admitting that you are not strong enough to do this alone. Quite the contrary, there is great strength and encouragement to be found in linking arms with others who care about you and your family. Regardless if that care comes from another adoptive parent who understands what you are going through, a non-judgmental family member, a physician, psychiatrist, pastor, or someone else, these people can be seen as the grace of God's hand giving you the provisions you need to make it through the wilderness.

'I will make a way in the wilderness and rivers in the desert.' This verse in Isaiah not only declares God's active presence in our day-to-day encounters, but it also points us forward to an even greater help in our lives, the salvation we can find in Christ alone. Speaking of Himself to the lady at the well, Jesus said in John 4:13-14, *'Everyone who drinks this water will be thirsty again, but whoever drinks the water I give them will never thirst. Indeed, the water I give them will become in them a spring of water welling up to eternal life.'* This living water is unlike any other. It is available to us who love Him, and to our children. Yes, we may have our own deserts to travel through on our way to wherever it is that God is leading us, but we must not become discouraged. God, you see, is doing a mighty work through us and in us as we travel across those arid lands. He is reminding us daily that because we are His children, He will not leave us and our families as captives. Instead, He will bring us into freedom: freedom in Christ who died on the cross to release us from those things that keep us in bondage; freedom from the chains of sin; freedom from blindly going through life in darkness, apart from God; freedom from experiencing a life void of hope. This is the freedom found only at the foot of the cross.

Christ further spoke of Himself by quoting an Old Testament prophecy: *'He has sent me to proclaim freedom for the prisoners and recovery of sight for the blind, to set the oppressed free, to proclaim the year of the Lord's favor'* (Luke 4:18-19). With that freedom gushes the water we so desperately need to give life and nourishment to our weary souls. As we put our trust in Him, He fills us with rivers of living water and opens our eyes to see that He is all we need. He is doing a new thing in our lives. Rejoice! Trust that God can help us release expectations that the past will continually repeat itself. Look forward with great hope that God will not leave us to perish in the desert, but will see us through the entire journey to the end. And, just as He ushered my Granddaddy into heaven, one day, those of us who bow to Christ as Lord and Savior will enter into our new, glorious home. We must never lose sight of the fact that our lives here do not encompass all that God has planned for us. There is more! We must keep looking up, striving toward the finish line set for us.

Although we may want to have a living and active hope, some days, our deserts seem endless. No matter how hard we strain to look into the distance, we cannot make out the oasis prepared for us. I know that Jesus is the One who refreshes my soul and fills me with His eternal, living water. At times, though, I forget that I am already full of all I need, and I look desperately for a substitute. On those days, I am deflated, and my strength to carry on is weak.

I remember one particular Mother's Day, a year or so after we had adopted Carl, when I felt like a total, complete failure as a mom. Jeff had to go to church early that day, so he and the boys left first. When my daughters and I piled into the other car, I found that I could not leave the driveway, for I

157

was crying too hard to see the road. My girls tried to console me, but nothing seemed to help. My heart was breaking, for the relationship I longed to have with Carl seemed to be an impossible dream. In fact, for a number of reasons, the relationship I had with *both* of my sons at that point was strained, and it looked as if I was losing both of them at the same time, though in different ways. Finally, I pulled myself together enough to drive to church, but I could not make myself go inside. I just couldn't, for I knew that during the service, there would be a time of honor for the mothers in the church. I usually cherish this particular day, for all the children are invited to go to the front of the church where they can choose a flower to bring back and give to their mothers. It is such a sweet gesture, and the children enjoy giving like that. How could I sit in the celebration this year, though, knowing I was failing them? I just couldn't do it. I didn't think I deserved any flowers or recognition, especially not then. I did not feel worthy of celebration.

So, after I dropped the girls off, I found a parking space as far away from the door as I could. Not only was the spot a good distance from the entrance, but it was also on the opposite side from where we normally parked. I didn't want anyone to find me. I sat there and tried to pray, but couldn't seem to get past the tears of regret and sorrow. As time clicked by, I began to think about what was going on inside the church. I imagined all five of my children going up front to get flowers and then bringing them back to an empty chair instead of to their mother. That made me cry all the more. I was spiraling down, and I felt there was no way back up.

Not long after that, I noticed Jeffery, my younger son, coming out the front door all by himself. He looked over at our normal parking space and did not see our car. I thought for sure he would go back inside, but he didn't. Instead, he looked until he found me. He walked over to where I was, quietly opened the passenger door, and sat down beside me. Then he handed me the flower he had acquired in the service, along with a card he had made, telling me that he loved me. He hugged me and said everything was going to be alright. Then he beckoned me to come inside for the end of the service. How could I say no?

Jeffery had no idea how much his compassion meant to me that day. His effort to reach out gave me a ray of hope that all was not lost. So, I took a deep breath and went inside with my son. As I walked in, the congregation was standing, singing the last song before the close of the service. Before I made it to the row where my family was, Madison saw Jeffery and me walking in. I saw her turn to her siblings to tell them that we were coming. They all turned to look at me. Then something unexpected and refreshing happened. Rather than waiting for me to approach them, they burst out from the row and made their way to me, offering hugs and words of love. Even Carl came over and shyly hugged me, giving me the flower he had been clutching.

I could see Jesus' love shining through my children …
Springs of water bubbling up in my little desert.

That day marked another turning point for me, for it became abundantly evident that God was at work in our family even when we felt as worn down as if we had been walking through a literal desert. God was well aware that the past year had been extremely difficult, and that I was feeling weak and ineffective. Through these acts of love from my children when I was at my lowest, God gave me the strength to persevere. He broke through the chains of despair and replaced them with rivers of hope. Hope for a better future. Hope for continued family relationships. Hope for a renewed, strengthened heart for Carl.

Now, a few years past that emotional Mother's Day, I can say that Carl and I have a mother-son relationship that is growing in the right direction. I am humbled at how much God has taught me, and continues to teach me, about how amazing Carl is, how to better reach him, and how to touch his life in meaningful ways. He still has a long way to go in order to heal from his past traumas, but he is definitely progressing in healthy directions. He is realizing now that he can trust us. His relationship with his siblings is growing stronger. And he is learning about the importance of God in his life. I pray daily for Carl, and hang onto the hope I have that God is working in his life in ways that will ultimately draw him to salvation. Many days, though, I wonder why God is taking so long to soften Carl's heart, because I believe that

- Carl's life will heal more quickly once he begins to cling to Christ as his Lord and Savior.

- His heart will be lighter when he can extend forgiveness to his first parents, just as Christ forgives him.

- His perspective in life will change when he begins to operate out of a belief that God created him for specific plans and purposes.

- And his relationships in every arena of life will grow stronger when he learns the value of 'loving your neighbor as yourself,' which can only flow out of loving God with all your heart, mind, and soul (Mark 12:30-31).

Not long ago, in the middle of a church service, I started to become fearful that Carl would never accept Christ as his Lord and Savior. 'Shouldn't it have happened by now, Lord?' Statistics say that once a child gets older than the age of thirteen, if he has not yet become a Christian, chances are he never will, and Carl is almost sixteen! What if his heart doesn't change by the time he leaves home in just a few short years? Will he be forever lost? It's interesting how my thoughts can digress so quickly. As my anxiety over Carl's salvation increased, God softly prompted me to pick up my Bible and to read Zephaniah 3:17, replacing the pronouns with Carl's name:

The Lord your God is with [Carl],
the Mighty Warrior who saves.
He will take great delight in [Carl];
in his love he will no longer rebuke [Carl],
but will rejoice over [Carl] with singing.

In an instant, those words calmed my fearful heart and reignited my hope for Carl. God is surely with him, and He has the great power to save my son's soul from the grips of death. Not only that, but God reminded me how much He already loves Carl—so much so that He rejoices and sings over him! My eyes were opened to the reality that God delights in the fact that He made Carl, and that His plan is being worked out in His perfect timing. I am not to fear, but to rejoice that God has already brought Carl out from a cold, hard, lonely life as an orphan and placed him in a family who cherishes him. Why should I think that God will stop there?

As I thought about that, great hope swelled up in me that God is, indeed, saving Carl. He purposefully put him in a family who loves the Lord so that we could teach Carl the truths that he needs to know. Certainly, the Lord did not bring Carl this far in life to leave him in the darkness of existing apart from God. No, I have chosen to believe that God is, even now, at this very moment, working out His perfect plan to draw Carl to Himself, into the Light.

As I was silently rejoicing in the work of God in Carl's life, the church began to sing the song, 'Mighty to Save.' As I sang, tears began to stream down my cheeks, for God is, indeed, mighty to save my son, who has endured so much in life. There is no heart too hard for God to soften, no person too far away for God to find, and no life too difficult for Him to save.

> *Savior, he can move the mountains.*
> *My God is mighty to save,*
> *He is mighty to save.*
> *Forever author of salvation,*
> *He rose and conquered the grave,*
> *Jesus conquered the grave.*

(© 2006 Ben Fielding/Reuben Morgan/Hillsong Publishing (adm. in the U.S. and Canada by Integrity's Hosanna! Music)/ASCAP)

As new hope surged through me, I glanced over at Carl, who was standing two people down from me. Catching my glimpse, he looked my way, mouthing the words: 'I love this song!' I nodded in agreement, and finished singing …

So take me as you find me,
All my fears and failures,
Fill my life again.

I give my life to follow,
Everything I believe in,
Now I surrender.

'Yes, Lord, I give my own life to you, and I surrender my son to Your care. Help me to continue to see the great hope that only comes from You, Lord. Through the good days and the bad, You are always present, even when I cannot see or feel You. Thank You for that. Thank You that Carl's salvation is not dependent on my perfect actions, but on Yours. Be with us all, Lord, and help us to forever keep our eyes and hope on You, for You *can*, indeed, *"move the mountains"* that seem immoveable to us. You are *"mighty to save,"* and You *do* have a future destination planned for us. Ignite our hearts for You, Lord, so that even in the middle of the desert we can cling to the hope we have in You, and give You praise. I pray that You bubble up springs of water in us, and all around us. And may our response to You be one of complete trust, deep gratitude, and heart-felt worship. For, Lord, You are our all-in-all. You are everything we need. And we praise You.'

Give thanks to the LORD, for he is good;
*   his love endures forever.*

When hard pressed, I cried to the LORD;
*   he brought me into a spacious place.*

The LORD is with me; I will not be afraid.
The LORD is with me; he is my helper.

I was pushed back and about to fall,
     but the LORD helped me.
The LORD is my strength and my defense;
     he has become my salvation.

Shouts of joy and victory
     resound in the tents of the righteous:
The LORD's right hand has done mighty things!
The LORD's right hand is lifted high;
     the LORD's right hand has done mighty things!
I will not die but live,
     and will proclaim what the LORD has done.

I will give you thanks, for you answered me;
     you have become my salvation.
The stone the builders rejected
     has become the cornerstone;
the LORD has done this,
     and it is marvelous in our eyes.
The LORD has done it this very day;
     let us rejoice today and be glad.

You are my God, and I will praise you;
     you are my God, and I will exalt you.
Give thanks to the LORD, for he is good;
     his love endures forever.

PSALM 118:1, 5, 6a, 7a, 13-17, 21-24, 28-29

~⊗~

Personal Reflections:

1. Read Romans 8:24-25. In the midst of challenging days, is it difficult for you to hold on to hope? I encourage you to pray that the Holy Spirit will continually fill your heart and mind with the belief and hope that God is working, even when you cannot see what He is doing. Pray for endurance and patience to go the distance He is calling you to complete.

2. Read Isaiah 43:18-19. Do you believe that God is working a 'new thing' in your life and in the life of your child? Believe that God's words are true when He tells you He is making a way in the wilderness and will bring about rivers in the desert. How does this verse speak to you personally?

3. Read John 4:13-14. What does it mean that when we drink the water Christ gives us, we will never be thirsty again? How does this affect the way you view and live life?

4. Read Luke 4:18-19. This verse speaks directly to Christ's freeing His followers from spiritual death, blindness, and bondage. Can you identify specific areas in your own life where Christ has brought you freedom? Do you believe that your adopted child can also be delivered from the clutches of sin and death? How does this give you hope?

5. Read Zephaniah 3:17. As you read this verse, allow the beauty of our Lord's love to permeate your heart. Imagine Him smiling over your child, delighting in him. Then go

a step further, and remember that God loves your child so much that He actually rejoices over him with singing! Be assured that if God loves and rejoices over your child this much, then surely He is also working in His life in the best possible ways.

6. Read Psalm 118. Read it again, slowly this time. Allow the Holy Spirit to speak to you. Bask in the goodness of our Lord. Praise Him for who He is, and for His active involvement in your life and the life of your family. Pray that as you walk through the desert, He will bring you to a place of praise and worship. May your days be filled with hope, and your soul with rivers of living water.

Other books of interest from

Christian Focus Publications

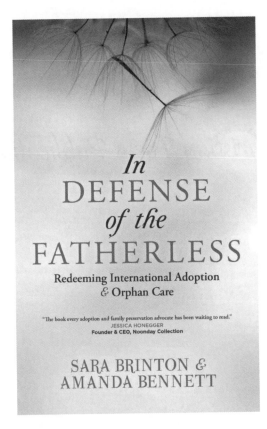

In
DEFENSE
of the
FATHERLESS

Redeeming International Adoption
& Orphan Care

"The book every adoption and family preservation advocate has been waiting to read."
JESSICA HONEGGER
Founder & CEO, Noonday Collection

SARA BRINTON &
AMANDA BENNETT

ISBN 978-1-78191-551-6

In Defense of the Fatherless

Redeeming International Adoption & Orphan Care

SARA BRINTON & AMANDA BENNETT

...will challenge, convict and fuel a conversation that is much needed today for the church to move forward in international adoption and orphan care passionately, wisely, and ethically.

JASON KOVACS,
Co-founder of Together for Adoption, Austin, Texas

...makes us all ask the questions: are we, as the church, caring for orphans and vulnerable children well? And how can we be doing better?

MEGAN PARKER,
Co-Founder, Abide Family Center, Jinja, Uganda

...the book every adoption and family preservation advocate has been waiting to read.

JESSICA HONEGGER,
Founder and CEO, Noonday Collection, Austin, Texas

This book should be on the 2015 reading list for all those in church leadership.

STEVE TIMMIS,
Executive Director of the Acts 29 Network & Pastor,
The Crowded House, Sheffield

Any couple thinking of adopting, any church wanting to be involved in solving this problem should read this book.

MARY WHELCHEL,
Director of Women's Ministries, The Moody Church, Chicago, Illinois

Sara Brinton is a writer and social entrepreneur who lives in Austin, Texas with her husband and their four children, including daughter Gabrielle who was adopted from Uganda. Amanda Bennett is a lawyer living in in Kigali, Rwanda with her husband and son.

THE
ENVY
OF Eve

FINDING CONTENTMENT IN
A COVETOUS WORLD

MELISSA B. KRUGER

ISBN 978-1-84550-775-6

The Envy of Eve

Finding Contentment in a Covetous World

MELISSA B. KRUGER

With empathy and grounded biblical insight, Melissa Kruger shows us the path to abiding joy amidst life's varied 'ups' and 'downs'.

LYDIA BROWNBACK,
Author of *Contentment*, Wheaton, Illinois

With I've-been-there understanding and been-in-the-Word insight, Melissa Kruger helps us to look beneath the surface of our discontent, exposing our covetous hearts to the healing light of God's Word.

NANCY GUTHRIE,
author of *Seeing Jesus in the Old Testament* Bible Study Series

Through biblical examples and sympathetic counsel we are pointed again and again to the delivering power of the Lord Jesus Christ.

FAITH COOK,
author of *Troubled Journey,* Derbyshire, England

In an age and culture where we all tend to have an overdeveloped sense of entitlement, this book makes a brilliant diagnosis that goes right to the heart of the problem.

ANN BENTON,
Author and family conference speaker, Guildford, England.

Melissa B. Kruger serves as Women's Ministry Coordinator at Uptown Church in Charlotte, North Carolina. Her husband, Michael J. Kruger, is the president of Reformed Theological Seminary in Charlotte.

HURT
FEELINGS
WRONG
ATTITUDES
COMPARING
YOURSELF TO OTHERS
GUILT
AFRAID TO
TRUST GOD
LETTING GO AND
MOVING ON WITH GOD

MARY WHELCHEL

GET
OVER
IT!

ISBN 978-1-78191-145-7

Get Over It!

Letting Go and Moving on with God

MARY WHELCHEL

Unrealistic expectations. Hurt feelings. False guilt. As we go about our daily lives, we are so often mired down in all kinds of joy-robbing thought patterns and unhealthy habits. But grounded in God's Word, we can move on, set free from these burdens.

Read this book and then pass it along to others who need to quit wallowing in their past-no matter how terrible it might be-and unload the baggage they have carried far too long.

Erwin Lutzer,
Senior Pastor, Moody Church, Chicago, Illinois

With the candor of a faithful friend, Mary Whelchel encourages us to get over our petty fears, attitudes and anxieties that prevent us from living freely and becoming all that God intends for us to be. Drawing on years of ministry experience, Whelchel provides practical advice and wisdom to fight our tendency to hold onto slights, guilt and unrealistic expectations.

Melissa B. Kruger,
Conference speaker, Women's Ministry Coordinator,
Uptown Church, Charlotte, North Carolina

Mary Whelchel draws from her own journey with God and her years of ministry to shepherd readers to the place of letting go of burdens we weren't meant to carry and courageously moving forward with God.

Carolyn Custis James,
Author of *Half the Church*

Mary Whelchel is founder of The Christian Working Woman, a ministry dedicated to equipping and encouraging Christians in the workplace.

SUSANNA WESLEY ◦ FANNY CROSBY

VANCE CHRISTIE

WOMEN *of*
FAITH
& COURAGE

CATHERINE BOOTH ◦ MARY SLESSOR ◦ CORRIE TEN BOOM

Women of Faith and Courage

Susanna Wesley, Fanny Crosby, Catherine Booth,
Mary Slessor and Corrie Ten Boom

MARY WHELCHEL

Thank you, Vance Christie, for your amazing biographies of five remarkable Christian women in history. Your book, *Women of Faith and Courage*, shows in a beautifully-written and fascinating style, the faithful devotion of these women for Christ, and allows us to look deeply into their lives and ministries. I can highly recommend this book, and I hope women around the world will study it for personal spiritual growth and also in a group Bible study setting. Truly, these five women are role models for all of us today!

DENISE GEORGE,
Author, teacher, speaker, www.denisegeorge.org

Whether confronted with poverty, a self-centered husband, endless debt, physical disabilities, perennial illness, government persecution, destructive fires, or loneliness, they all found faith in Christ gave them a courage to overcome every obstacle and serve Him.

DIANA LYNN SEVERANCE,
A historian with broad experience teaching in universities and seminaries,
Spring, Texas

This fascinating book, *Women of Faith and Courage*, shows in a beautifully-written and fascinating style, the faithful devotion of these women for Christ, and allows us to look deeply into their lives and ministries."

FAITH COOK,
author of *Troubled Journey*, Derbyshire, England

Vance Christie is a pastor and author best known for vivid re-telling of missionary stories. He lives in Aurora, Nebraska.

Christian Focus Publications

Our mission statement –

STAYING FAITHFUL
In dependence upon God we seek to impact the world through literature faithful to His infallible Word, the Bible. Our aim is to ensure that the Lord Jesus Christ is presented as the only hope to obtain forgiveness of sin, live a useful life and look forward to heaven with Him.

Our books are published in four imprints:

CHRISTIAN
FOCUS

Popular works including biographies, commentaries, basic doctrine and Christian living.

CHRISTIAN
HERITAGE

Books representing some of the best material from the rich heritage of the church.

MENTOR

Books written at a level suitable for Bible College and seminary students, pastors, and other serious readers. The imprint includes commentaries, doctrinal studies, examination of current issues and church history.

CF4•K

Children's books for quality Bible teaching and for all age groups: Sunday school curriculum, puzzle and activity books; personal and family devotional titles, biographies and inspirational stories – because you are never too young to know Jesus!

Christian Focus Publications Ltd,
Geanies House, Fearn, Ross-shire,
IV20 1TW, Scotland, United Kingdom.
www.christianfocus.com